André Theuriet

Song Birds and Seasons

André Theuriet

Song Birds and Seasons

ISBN/EAN: 9783337020057

Printed in Europe, USA, Canada, Australia, Japan

Cover: Foto ©Thomas Meinert / pixelio.de

More available books at **www.hansebooks.com**

Song Birds and Seasons

BY

ANDRÉ THEURIET

ILLUSTRATED BY HECTOR GIACOMELLI

BOSTON
ESTES AND LAURIAT

Copyright, 1888,
BY ESTES AND LAURIAT.

PRESSWORK BY JOHN WILSON AND SON.
UNIVERSITY PRESS.

LIST OF ILLUSTRATIONS.

SYMPHONY OF SPRING.

		PAGE
Border . .	Goldfinch, bullfinch, greenfinch, warblers	ix
Headpiece . .	The concert . .	xi
Initial Illustration	Finch in its bower	xi
Tailpiece .	Wren	xvi

THE FINCH.

Border	Young finches	1
Headpiece and Initial Illustration	Finch calling its little ones	3
Full-page Illustration .	The finch and its nest	7
Tailpiece	The finch of Ardennes	10

THE WARBLER.

Border	Young warblers	11
Headpiece and Initial Illustration	The open bills	13
Full-page Illustration . . .	Black-headed warbler . . .	17
Tailpiece	Warbler's nest	20

THE NIGHTINGALE.

Border .	Young nightingales .	21
Headpiece . .	Hymn to the moon .	23
Initial Illustration .	Song of love .	23
Full-page Illustration .	The nightingale .	27
Tailpiece . .	Warbler's nest .	30

THE GOLDFINCH.

		PAGE
Border .	The first flight	31
Headpiece . .	The nest	33
Initial Illustration	Goldfinch picking a thistle	33
Full-page Illustration . .	Goldfinch	37
Tailpiece . .	The galley-slave	40

THE LINNET AND THE SISKIN.

Border . .	Young linnets . .	41
Headpiece . . .	On the hedge .	43
Initial Illustration .	The first eggs .	43
Full-page Illustration .	Linnet's nest . .	47
Tailpiece .	The siskin .	50

THE GOLDHAMMER.

Border .	The nest and nestlings	51
Headpiece . .	The sorb-apples	53
Initial Illustration .	The cherries	53
Full-page Illustration .	The goldhammer	57
Tailpiece .	Female goldhammer	60

THE KING-FISHER.

Border . . .	The young of the king-fisher . . .	61
Headpiece . . .	The ambuscade	63
Initial Illustration	King-fisher diving	63
Full-page Illustration .	King-fisher	67
Tailpiece .	A good prey	70

THE SPARROW.

Border .	Young sparrows	71
Headpiece .	The assembly	73
Initial Illustration .	On the roof	73
Full-page Illustration .	In the fields	77
Tailpiece .	The hedge-sparrow . . .	80

THE WAGTAIL.

		PAGE
Border	Young wagtails	81
Headpiece and Initial Illustration	At the bath	83
Full-page Illustration .	Water-wagtail	87
Tailpiece . .	Yellow wagtail	90

THE STONE-CHAT.

Border	The stone-chat's song	91
Headpiece	Ploughed land	93
Initial Illustration	At the edge of the field . . .	93
Full-page Illustration	Hedge stone-chat's nest . . .	97
Tailpiece	Heath stone-chat . . .	100

THE NUT-HATCH AND THE LESSER WOODPECKER.

Border	The nut-hatches	101
Headpiece and Initial Illustration	The purveyors of the little birds . .	103
Full-page Illustration	The nut-hatch	107
Tailpiece	The woodpecker	110

THE LARK.

Border	The lark's little ones	111
Headpiece and Initial Illustration	Morning	113
Full-page Illustration . . .	Lark soaring	117
Tailpiece .	The young brood	120

THE RED-START.

Border	In the nest	121
Headpiece and Initial Illustration	The siesta	123
Full-page Illustration .	The red-start	127
Tailpiece . .	The blue-breast	130

THE BULLFINCH.

		PAGE
Border .	The nest	131
Headpiece . .	On the branches	133
Initial Illustration	Young bullfinches . .	133
Full-page Illustration	Bullfinches on the wing .	137
Tailpiece	Twee-twee-twee	140

THE THRUSH.

Border	On the watch	141
Headpiece and Initial Illustration	On the vine	143
Full-page Illustration .	The thrush	147
Tailpiece .	The mavis	150

THE SWALLOW.

Border	Young swallows	151
Headpiece and Initial Illustration	A telegraph wire . . .	153
Full-page Illustration	In the open sky .	157
Tailpiece	Dead . .	160

THE RED-BREAST.

Border . .	Young red-breasts	. 161
Headpiece . .	In quest of shelter .	163
Initial Illustration .	The nest	163
Full-page Illustration .	First snow . .	. 167
Tailpiece .	Leaving the nest .	. 170

THE TITMOUSE FAMILY.

Border . .	Young blue titmice .	. 171
Headpiece .	Winter	. 173
Initial Illustration . .	Great titmouse	. 173
Full-page Illustration .	Great black headed titmouse	. 177
Tailpiece	Crested titmouse	180

THE WREN AND THE TROGLODYTE.

		PAGE
Border .	A prey	. . 181
Headpiece . . .	Wrens (the rivals)	. . 183
Initial Illustration .	Wren and her little ones	. . 185
Full page Illustration . . .	Wren's nest	 187
Tailpiece	Troglodyte	. . 190

THE BLACKBIRD.

Border	Young blackbirds	. 191
Headpiece . . .	Across the fields	. 193
Initial Illustration .	On the branches	. 195
Full-page Illustration	Spring shower	. 197
Tailpiece	The ouzel	. 200

A SYMPHONY

Feathered guests of the wood and wold,
Singers who pipe in copse and mead;
Blackbird of jet and finch of gold;
Warbler, rocked by the wind-swept reed;
And you, O wonderful nightingale,
The only poet with wings endowed,
And you, sweet lark from the grassy dale,
Hanging in heaven, high in the cloud.

Hail, O nation of folks with wings,
Cleaving the air in your rapid flight!
Men are glad when the season brings
Ye to your homes in the branches light
Singers whose bridal music floats
Skyward, blent with the scent of flowers,
Angel voices, whose joyful notes
Soothe these sorrowing hearts of ours!

A SYMPHONY OF SPRING

At first an almost insensible rustling, a scarcely perceptible thrill runs through the forest, like the mysterious murmur of growing grass, of opening leaves and of rising sap; — then, on the skirt of the coppice where the yellow cornelian-tree is in full bloom, at the bottom of the moist valleys where the laurel unfurls its pink corolla, three notes burst forth, three joyous, quick, sharp redoubled notes: it is the first awakening of the songsters of the woods, the blackbird that whistles his merry song to the newly budding trees, like a boy let out of school shouting to all the nooks of the forest : « Merrily! merrily! let us enjoy ourselves ; spring has come back ; to-day is Saint-Alban's day, when every bird has chosen the place of its nest! » Two voices respond to this merry companion : one, at the same time soft and thrilling bursts forth from the shadiest coverts, 't is that of the finch ; — the other, clear, wild and joyful is that of the black-cap. These two new-comers sing but a short strain, but they repeat it to satiety, as if they felt the need of convincing themselves that winter is really gone and that in spite of April showers spring has not been countermanded.

Down below, in the plain where wheat and rye are growing green, hundreds of aerial, melodious voices confirm this good news. It is the morning chorus of sky-larks. At break of day, the first one awake soars upwards rising in a straight line as high as possible, like the sailor on the outlook at the top of the highest mast, and proclaims to all its kind that the season of love and nest building has come; then it falls straight down like the plumb line into the grassiest furrows. Another skylark soars upwards, then a third, then twenty others; you can hardly perceive them up above in the rosy purple of the rising sun ; but you can hear their distant melody, the notes of which seem to drop down like shining pearls from a string.

The signal for the concert is now given. From every nook and corner, from the hedges on the road-side, from the full-blown fruit trees of the orchard, from the low banks of the river, from the shady glens of the forest, a marvellous ensemble fills the resonant atmosphere: the trills of the goldfinch, the chirping of the linnet and the titmouse, the runs of the thrush, the tremolo of the hoopoo, the interlude of the bullfinch, the soft shrill of the wren and the nut-hatch. Then, at intervals, breaking in upon this unceasing variety of sound, two grave deep, dreamy, redoubled notes ring through the thickness of the forest.

It is the voice of the cuckoo, that invisible, fanciful singer that you hear almost at the same time in all the nooks and corners of the wood, and his song seems to rythm the flight of time. You think him quite near, you seek him and suddenly his sonorous appeal bursts forth from afar. It is he who throws a melancholy note into this concert of universal joy. This full and mysterious double note, which ever seems to die away and which constantly resounds again, is like an echo of vanished springs and of forgotten friendships. It seems to sigh: « Remember! remember! Give a thought to those who have gone for ever, to the memory of those beloved beings who can no more taste the rapture of the revival of nature. Time flies and carries you along... For you also, spring will not bloom always! » But in spite of the prognostics of this melancholy, capricious warner, the joyful merriment of the light-hearted tribe bursts forth ever and anon in an exuberance of song. Leaves are growing, lilies of the valley perfume the air, nests are being built everywhere: in the grass, in the hedges, in the hollow of dead trees, in the branches of green boughs, and every one thinks only of the delights of the present hour.

Now the black and white swallows, with their pointed, arrow-like wings, come out of all the streets of the village. These fearless travellers come from afar and manifest their joy of being home again by the most astonishing circuits. Air-drinkers as they are, they brush past the top of roofs, skim along the ground, disappear under the arches of the bridges and reappear suddenly in the bright sun-light; they veer about, rise, fly up and down without ever perching and hardly uttering the slightest sound. The silent dance of these black gypsies is like an intermezzo in the symphony of spring. It is the ballet in the middle of the concert.

Meanwhile yonder, in the forest, the singing continues. From the bottom of the thicket the cooing of the wild wood-pigeon, at once low and tender, loud and yet clouded comes towards us. The passionate, languishing note rises, falls, rises again; you seem to hear the sleepy forest utter unconscious sighs in its dream. This is no longer the joyous greeting of the sky-lark at early dawn, nor the sprightly prattle of the black-bird, nor the sonorous call of the cuckoo; it is the intimate talk of a loving married couple, who exchange tender and caressing vows, happy in their conjugal felicity. The wood-pigeons coo on heedless of their surroundings; they give themselves up to their mutual tenderness and like the lovers in La Fontaine's fable :

> *Ils se sont l'un à l'autre un monde toujours beau,*
> *Toujours divers, toujours nouveau...*

But now the shadows are lengthening on the fields; the sky reflects a deeper azure hue in the ponds; the thickets assume a redder tint and the first twinkling star trembles above the horizon. The voices grow fainter and fainter, the birds fall asleep near their nests. You would think that the concert is going to end, but it is only a temporary hush, a cleverly managed pause to prepare the entrance of the grand artist of spring.

The nightingale sings, and Nature herself seems to be listening. The admirable strains of this master soloist fill up the whole interval from night-fall to day-break. Beside him all other performers retire into shade; listening to him, you forget their humble songs, just as the sweet scented, milk-white lily of the valley obliterates the remembrance of April flowerets. With the song of the nightingale the enchantment of fairy-land begins to reign in the woods. His hymn is the song of tyrannical, violent, passionate, tender and sensuous love. You never grow tired of hearing this song, you would have it last forever.

But nothing lasts forever. Towards the middle of June the breath of the master artist grows shorter, and when the midsummer sun shines on the fields his powerful voice is no longer heard in the night. Earlier yet than he the warblers have ceased their song. One bird alone, the chattering warbler utters its deafening, vulgar melopœia, among the willows by the river bathed in sunshine; its noisy music rises above the glistening waters, above the transparent blaze of the fiery atmosphere, while down yonder, among the ripe cherries of the orchard the goldfinch drinks in the perfumed juice, scarcely able to throw out three flute-like, lisping notes. These are the last songsters of the season, and their sun-warmed strains end the « Symphony of spring ».

THE FINCH

Twit, twit! ... 't is the spring time now
There are finches on every bough.

Now winter is past and ended,
Their lay with the merle's is blended;
It tells the boys of Easter at hand,
　　With flowerets gay.

Dust in a shower golden
Falls from the willows olden,
Willows, whose flower we bear in hand
　　On Easter Day.

Hail, little finch of the woods wide,
Rejoicing loud in the springtide!
Youth, spring, the flower strewn land
　　Inspire thy lay.

　Twit! twit... 't is the spring time now
　There are finches on every bough!

THE FINCH

Taking a walk in the woods on one of the first fine days of March, I heard in the distance the merry song of a bird. At that time of the year the leafless forest has the sonority of an empty dwelling and that early song rang joyously through the woods like the forerunner of coming spring. The song consisted of three parts : a lively prelude, a trill and a final modulation with a powerful, delicate sound. I recognized the song of the finch, and that strain of early spring brought back to my mind a remembrance of childhood, which seemed to rise from afar, like the song, from the very depths of the forest.

At that time, being eleven years old, I used to lay snares for young birds in a coppice belonging to my grandfather. These snares are very common in the province of Lorraine, especially from September to November, the time of passage. All the small fry of birds are sure to be taken in these traps, especially in the cruel one that La Fontaine calls « *Rezinglette* » and which in our parts is called the « *Grasshopper* ».

This snare consists of a supple hazel switch curved like a racket, the two ends of which are brought together by a double cord. These rackets are placed edgewise along the paths or the ponds frequented by birds, every twenty feet. Some of the more skilled snarelayers even fasten a bunch of sorberries above the racket as a bait. Early in the morning and late at night, some sharp billed bird is sure to come and drink in the pond tempted by the treacherous appearance of that inviting perch; they settle on it, a peg comes down with a dry noise, and the poor creature is caught in the suddenly tightened slip knot and hangs suspended by its bruised members at the top of the unstrung racket.

One evening as my grandfather and I were taking our last walk, I heard some sharp cries in a footpath close by and I saw a bird just caught in one of our « *Grasshoppers* ». It was about the size of a sparrow and it fluttered so furiously that it had almost overset the racket. Nevertheless, it had not been injured, perhaps the cord had not snapped back as suddenly as usual, or the feet of the victim had been more resistant. Its back was chestnut-coloured, the top of its head and its bill bluish drab; it had bright eyes, black mustachios; its neck, breast and sides were of a fine wine colour, its rump of a dark olive shade; it had besides a forked tail and a white spot on each wing.

« It is a finch from the Ardennes, » said my grandfather. I knew it already, for having taken it by its wings so as to set it free, it had bitten me to the blood. My grandfather observed to me that its feet had not been broken, one only being slightly scratched. When I saw how lively and pretty it was, I thought I should like to put it into a case and tame it. I begged to be allowed to take it home and I insisted so well that the permission was granted. « Very well », said my grandfather, shaking his head; « but you will surely never be able to bring it up; it is already too strong and too wild ».

Of course I did not believe him, being at that presumptions age when we have no doubts about anything. I wrapped the finch up in my handkerchief and as soon as we got home I placed it in a well closed wicker basket until I could prepare a cage for it the next day.

I passed half the night without being able to sleep,

as the thought of my prisoner kept running in my head. I had heard that finches have a marvelous musical aptitude and that with patience one can train them to be regular artists; so that when my eyes closed at last, I heard my pupil singing in my dreams like the blue bird of fairy-land. At dawn I ran to my basket. The finch had scarcely slept better than I; it was fluttering about sullenly, pecking furiously at the sides of the basket. I spent all the money I had saved on a cage containing a trough and a manger which I filled with hempseed. I moved my bird into its cage and while it was getting accustomed to its new dwelling, I climbed into our garret, where I consulted some old volumes on ornithology, so as to get well acquainted with the habits and tastes of my guest.

There I learned that finches are naturally very merry, that they sing early in the spring, long before the nightingale, and that besides their regular song, they throw out three peculiar notes: a cry of appeal at the time of courtship, a war cry when they fight against a rival, and finally, when it is going to rain, a long wail which is a certain prognostic of bad weather. I saw besides that finches build their nests in the most thickly spreading trees; these nests are round, solidly woven of moss on the outside, of hair and spider-webs on the inside; the female lays five or six red brown eggs spotted with black at the broader

THE FINCH

end; the male remains patiently near his mate, feeding their young with insects and caterpillars; my author added that adult finches feed on seeds, such as poppies, mast and grain.

Thus well informed, I returned to the cage. The prisoner did not at all seem inclined to get used to it. Clutching at the bars, fluttering incessantly, he had upset the trough and disdained the hemp-seed which filled the manger. I thought perhaps the bird did not like its fare, my book having spoken of poppies and mast. I ran into the fields to search for this food; when I came back the feverish agitation of the prisoner had redoubled. It continued throwing itself against the bars in a state of great rage, bruising its pretty bluish head, breaking the feathers of its tail, while the bristled down of its chest was flying about the air. From time to time, being out of breath it would huddle itself up in a corner, opening wide its deep black eyes and its despairing glance seemed to cry out to me : « Set me free! oh set me free! » I turned a deaf ear to its mute appeal and left it, beguiling myself with the hope that the night would calm it. At day-break I ran again to my cage... there lay the finch, already stiffened, on the bottom board of the cage, with closed eyelids, bristled dull plumage, dead amidst the scattered seeds it had left untouched. The wild bird of the mountain, hating its prison, had starved itself to death.

My heart failed me, for the cruel agony of the poor bird weighed on my conscience. For a long while I could not see a bird without feeling strangely uneasy. And to-day still, after so many years, while I was listening to the early trills of the finch in the brushwood, this remembrance of my childhood came back to my mind with the bitter taste of remorse.

THE WARBLER

When April scatters her flowerets few,
The leaves are green in the woodland bower,
Gay little warbler, we welcome you,
    Sweetly singing.

Down by the waters blue and clear,
Woven deftly 'twixt reed stalks three,
Hangs your nest, o'er the placid mere
    Softly swinging.

Wild and sweet is your rapid lay,
Passionate, brief. How the joys of youth,
Keen, and so swift to pass away,
    Are like your singing!

THE WARBLER

Of all sylvan birds the warbler is the one with which we are the most familiar. If we have ever lived in the country, we have surely known one or two. The tribe of warblers is numerous: the grey warbler, the black cap and the whole class of reed warblers that includes the great sedge warbler, the marsh warbler, and the white throat.

The grey warbler is the largest and most common of all. It generally lives in gardens, orchards, bean and pea fields. It perches on the sticks which sustain these creeping vegetables; there it plays its gambols and builds its nest. It remains there till harvest time.

which coincides generally with the period of migration. During the season of courtship and brooding these wreath and flower-covered boughs resound with light melodies, and these joyous marriage songs harmonize sweetly with the tender green of the peas, the delicate blossoms of which resemble a flight of white butterflies.

The black cap is the best known warbler and the most gifted as regards garb and song. When fully grown, its black hood covers the crown of its head and falls over its eyes; around the neck the plumage is slate coloured, getting lighter towards the chest, it is white on the breast with a slight shade of black; the back and wings are greyish brown, with a light olive tint.

The song of the black cap is sweet and sustained. It consists of a series of short, brisk and clear modulations; some rather louder notes are heard in the soft, sweet strain, then all is blended again in a soft twittering. It is truly the language of the first emotions in spring, at once lively and discreet. 't is the song of the youth of the year. When the quick joyous notes of the warbler resound in hazel and cherrytrees, school-boys say: "Winter is passing away," and suddenly playing truants, they wander about in bands, roving about the woods, basking in the sun, seeking for nests and cutting whistles in the willow branches moist with sap.

As for me, I can never hear the song of this warbler without remembering the whole series of rustic pleasures which the burden of its strain promised me in my turbulent childhood. It calls to my mind my father's garden with its thick border of raspberry bushes, its boxwood and juniper trees scattered about the walks. In the heart of one of these juniper trees, I discovered one morning the nest of a black cap warbler. Placed at the root of the branches, hardly two feet from the ground, it consisted on the outside of moss and dry grass, inside, of finely interwoven hair. This nest contained five light brown, spotted eggs with darker veins. I could not resist the naughty childish caprice of stealing one of the pretty spotted eggs. The next day when I came to watch the brooding mother, I found that the eggs were broken and the nest abandoned.

Warblers are unmanageable on this point ; as soon as the hand of a stranger has broken in upon the mystery of their nest, considering the intrusion of this unknown enemy as an ill omen for their future family, they prefer destroying the whole, beginning to lay their eggs elsewhere where the brood will be less unlucky. Both father and mother watch their progeniture with equal solicitude, relieving each other to brood and showing an attachment to their newly hatched young which lasts as long as the season. They keep their young fledglings near them. You can see them flying about the skirt of the woods, the father ahead as a scout; if he perceives an abundant harvest of wild gooseberries or elderberries in the bushes, he gives notice of it to his family by a joyous *couic*, and the whole troop hastens thither to partake of the feast.

The habits of the reed-warblers are very different. The great sedge warbler prefers dwelling among swampy wooded banks; the marsh-warbler prefers gardens and fields near running water; the white throat prefers to dwell among the willows near rye and hemp fields. There are some traits common to them all; they all have a flattened head like the swallow, a strong bill and a long and robust thumb nail; they all feed exclusively on those insects which abound in the neighbourhood of water; they all have the same yellowish grey plumage and the same shrill, sharp notes in their song.

Their deep nests are artistically built, skilfully woven on the outside and inside with dry supple grasses. They generally suspend them on two or three stems tied together by as many rings of moss and hair; these moveable loops are loose enough to allow the nest to rise and fall according to the height of the waters.

In this aerial dwelling which the current and the slightest breeze sway to and fro, the female lays five cream coloured eggs, veined with brown. As soon as the eggs are laid, she does not again leave her nest, but allows it

THE WARBLER

to be rocked; whilst the male, perching on a willow branch or clinging to a reed, goes on repeating all day his joyous sprightly song, letting the quick, shrill notes succeed each other with unvaried regularity:—cri, cri, cra, cara, cara!

The sun shoots down its rays, and between the reeds the water has the dazzling glare of molten silver; the fiery atmosphere seems to blaze, and that monotonous unceasing song harmonizes with the twinkling of the river, the buzzing of the insects and the quavering of the hot air. It is a continual babbling, harsh like the voice of a busy housewife as she comes and goes about the house, giving her orders, scolding her servants and never stopping her chattering. In the district of *Brie*, in France, they say of a talkative woman, she chatters like a white throat. *(Elle jase comme une effarvatte.)*

This merry warbler has all the domestic virtues of a good housewife, but her faults as well: exclusive, positive and domineering, she wishes above all to be mistress in her own house, and will allow no other birds to settle in the place she has chosen. But it is a good-natured bird after all. In the long summer days, in the gloomy neighbourhood of solitary ponds, it throws out now and then a joyful note. Its song has a rather common melody, it is lively and free, like the merriment of the mob. In spite of its unvaried trite modulations, it is rather original. Whoever has once heard it will never forget it. It mingles with the impression left by fine summer days in flowery fields, just as the noisy burden of the belated labourer's song blends with the touching remembrance of a poetical night in spring.

THE NIGHTINGALE

When haply, wandering over hill and dale,
I in the woods have heard the nightingale,
Meseems that long and deeply I have quaffed
The potent magic of some wizard draught,
Drawn from all wondrous herbs of mystic might,
And woodland fragrance. With what keen delight
His song mounts higher, towards the sky!

If, borne on elfin wings, pursuing, I
Could follow, higher yet and yet more high,
Methinks, my heart, that I might find above
What was, in days of old,—lost youth, lost love.
Time hath no part, O wondrous bird, with thee.
Thine is today the self-same melody
That echoed in the woods when time was young.

Kings of the ancient earth have heard it sung.
Nor is it changed because their hearts, of old
Glad with the song, are silent now and cold.
Immortal is thy song, because its spring
Is love; which is eternal—therefore, Sing!

THE NIGHTINGALE

This is the master artist, the very king of singing birds. It is small in size, greyish white and reddish brown in garb, it makes no outward show and ought never to be seen but from the distance. It needs the soft twilight of the moon, the mystery of the leafy forest or the darkness of night; but beneath that more than humble garb is hidden a poet's nature, a most passionate soul, served by a most marvelous instrument.

Already in the sixteenth century did old Belon become almost lyrical in speaking of the nightingale: « When the trees of the forest are covered with green, the nightingale for a long while, ceases its song neither by day nor by night. Does there exist a man so deprived of judgment as not to be struck with admiration at hearing such a sweet, loud strain coming out of the throat of such a small wild bird? The best of the nightingale is that it persists so obstinately in its song, without ever getting tired or interrupting its strain; it would rather cease to live than cease to sing. »

It makes its appearance in our gardens and woods at the end of April when all Nature is busy with the work of love and reproduction. Its beautiful song ceases about the middle of June. It comes from the land of the ever fiery sun; there it learned those warm, metallic notes which seem to us the echo of the bright, glowing East. The extent of its voice is surprising, and yet more marvelous is the robust constitution of this frail little bird that can sing on, night after night. Also this artist requires a special food : no seeds, no watery debilitating fruit, but live, and so to say bleeding flesh. It lives exclusively on worms, insects and the larvae of ants. Like most singers it is a great eater, but a great eater of food that is rich in nitrogen. By means of this strengthening nourishment, its muscles acquire a wonderful strength and its voice unequalled volume and sound.

It chooses some sonorous glade or some solitary old tree where to give its concert, and twilight or the silent night for the hour of its representation. (Thence its name of nightingale : the songster of the night. Every thing in this bird betrays an artist's temperament, every thing, even the refined arrangement of its nest, composed outwardly of leaves that are superposed like the petals of a rose, and lined on the inside with long, slender, narrow blades of grass, artistically interwoven. The female nightingale lays three or five shining, greenish brown eggs; while she is performing the office of brooding the male is perched on a neighbouring tree, charming the long hours of her sitting with exquisite melodies.

It is not the performance of a skilful and cold virtuoso, but the passionate hymn of a fiery, voluptuous soul. The Germans, who are apt to be pedantic even in poetry, have tried to transcribe the song of the nightingale and one of their learned ornithologists, M. Bechtein, has made a syllabic notation of it. This is like trying to give and idea of the perfume of the rose by means of a chemical formula. Why attempt to render by insufficient human sounds that divine strain that every one has heard?

This ever varying, masterly melody is truly enchanting. It expresses every emotion : melancholy and joy, tenderness and passion. The song begins with some rapid, thrilling trills; then it changes slowly into a coaxing, tender lullaby, like an appeal to love; then the strain is broken by two deep, grave notes which die away like long sighs; then, again suddenly the tone of the artist changes : brillanti, trills, staccati, sparkling, sonorous flourishes, succeed each other rapidly, — and then again they all blend in a dim, dreamy melody. In that original strain, « In shadiest covert hid, » you seem to inhale the perfume of the lily of the valley and of sweet scented forest flowerets, the sap of budding leaves, the gushing joy of life in its full bloom.

When I was twenty years old and living in a village, how many nights I passed leaning on the open window-sill, listening to the song of the nightingales dispersed in the bowers! They responded by turns and seemed to vie with each other in eloquence and passion. All around, far and near, the orchards were plunged in mysterious darkness. I listened, charmed, spell-bound, as if I were living in fairy-land. To this ever varying, thrilling melody I would put unconnected words, such as one murmurs in a dream, and I felt myself lifted up, carried away in a magnificent current of poetry.

Even to day, when I spend the month of May in the country, it happens to me to listen at night to the amorous serenade of the nightingale, trying to recall the emotions and enchantment of by gone days. But alas! youth never comes back to those to whom it has once sung its « Song of songs ». Spring time returns, leaves grow green, nightingales breathe again their serenade in the blooming apple-trees, but other generations enjoy the feast and inhale the balmy breath, the intoxicating liquor of May! It is the same strain and the same fermentation of sap

THE NIGHTINGALE

in the forest, but the guests are not the same. Youth has invited other guests to sail in his flower-wreathed boat. Whilst we, the elder ones remain on the banks of the river, tired and disenchanted, the merry skiff sails away, and the chorus of the nightingales which it carries along, grows fainter and fainter as it disappears in the distance..... finally dying completely away in the darkness.....

It is not youth that dies away, it is we who disappear; the song of the nightingale is eternal, but where are the birds that sang it twenty years ago? The divine strain itself lasts but a short time every year, hardly two months from Saint-George's to Saint-John's day. After midsummer, the nightingale sings no more. The young are hatched and the cares and preoccupations of material existence put a stop to the poet's inspiration. Their notes are now harsh, being a sort of plaintive jarring, snapping noise; these last sounds seem intended for menace and defiance. The representation is over, the foot lights are put out, the marvelous artist leaves the scene of his triumphs, and carrying his starving brood away with him, he takes his flight towards neighbouring fields and bushes where he will find a more plentiful provision of worms. When you meet him by chance in autumn, fluttering widly across some solitary footpath, you will scarcely recognize in that silent bird with its livery of a dull brownish grey, the dazzling singer of those spell-bound May nights. It is then like those artists so animated and dazzling, apparently so young and brilliant when seen in the costume of the stage, the dim perspective of the back ground, and the sparkling footlights, and whom you are surprised to find so faded and old-looking, when you see them leave the theatre, clad in an old over-coat, tramping along pitifully in the mud.

THE GOLDFINCH

Come flowers or storms of sleet
Let me build in April, sweet,
A house for two.

Then in our tiny nest
Thy yellow wing shall rest
O'er eggs so blue.

At night, in tree top high
We'll watch the starry sky
Change in its hue,

When shines the morning chill
O'er distant dale and hill,
Reddening the blue.

It will not chill our nest!
Warmly and well may rest
Hearts warm and true!

THE GOLDFINCH

Like the goldhammer, the goldfinch is one of our rare singing birds whose smart costume harmonizes with its melodious, sonorous voice. Old Belon the naturalist says : « it is a bird of finer colour than any other we have in France. » Its pretty, arch little head is covered with a black hood which is joined by a black line to its ivory-coloured neck; the upper part of the face is covered by a sort of crimson velvet mask, through which two arch, dark brown eyes are glistening. Its whitish neck and breast of the same colour, its black wings spotted with gold, its brown back and spotted white tail, combine to make it a most impetuous and irresistible charmer.

> *Charmant, jeune, trainant tous les cœurs après soi.....*

Of course I am speaking of the male only; for the plumage of the female is duller and her habits more peaceful. She is the type of a housewife who loves her home, and she hardly ever leaves her carefully interwoven nest. This nest is at the same time solid and comfortable; outside, it is made of fine moss, lichen and thistle burrs, the whole interwoven with small roots; inside, it is like a soft elastic cushion made of hair, dry grass, feathers and wool. Goldfinches like to suspend their nests on to the most flexible boughs of fruit trees, so that the slightest breeze swings their aerial home gently to and fro. Sometimes, however, they build their nests on more steady ground, such as the hollow of a bush or the heart of a clump of green.

Last spring, I found two such nests built close together in the entangled boughs of some ivy covering an old garden wall. Each nest contained seven young ones, — seven greedy mouths which opened wide as soon as you put aside the ivy leaves. The two families seemed to be intimately united. Towards evening, the males would come together on a neighbouring lawn, smoothing their feathers and warbling their song with quaint motions of the head, just as respectable towns'people come together at nightfall after the day's work, in order to have a little gossip while enjoying the cool of the evening on their doorsteps. Meanwhile, the busy females were fluttering to and fro in search of flies and small worms for the supper of their large family.

One day it happened that the cat of the family, which had hidden treacherously behind a clump of lilac trees, took one of the mothers by surprise as she was leaving her nest, and strangled her. I then witnessed a most touching scene, which proves that charity is not exclusively a human virtue, and that it can dwell even in the heart of an humble goldfinch. The surviving mother adopted the children of the dead bird. She undertook to feed the two broods, and during a whole week, I used to see her flying from one nest to the other, dividing the food between her seven little ones and the seven orphans.

The female goldfinch is an honest, valiant creature; she is the very embodiment of self-denial and devotion; she shows a most exemplary attachment to her young ones; the sun may shine or the clouds burst in cold hail showers, she remains sitting on her nest with outspread wings, and sometimes after a storm, the hail has bruised her while she was faithfully attending to her tender brood.

Too fine to work, the male goldfinch, meanwhile, scarcely helps her in her task; he sometimes bends over the nest which contains the young ones and beguiles his faithful mate with the varied modulations of his clear song, his free and tender strain. This song consists in two strophes, or rather in a prelude and a cavatina, which are separately executed at longer or shorter intervals. The melodious cavatina is set off and enlivened by brilliant flourishes, in which one can distinguish three characteristic notes : Finch! Finch! Finch! which come back ever and anon like a roll-call. The male is very proud of his musical talent, just as he is intensely vain of his bright colours and brilliant plumage. He probably thinks that his beauty excuses him from demeaning himself with vulgar household cares, and he whiles away his time in self-indulgence, selfishness and voluptuous idleness.

When the young ones are fledged and feathered and strong enough to fly, the whole family takes its flight to the fields. The goldfinch is a high liver, an epicure, fond of choice and savoury seeds. In French this bird is called *chardonneret*, that is, a lover of thistles, but in spite of its name, it does not care for thistles, at least not until cold weather sets in ; then it is often obliged to be content with such meagre fare. In autumn, these pretty birds start off in flocks and go marauding about poppy and rape fields. Of a very quarrelsome disposition, they often have a fight with linnets, who haunt the same parts, but the goldfinches are generally victorious ; however, they also meet titmice and these birds, with

THE GOLDFINCH

their sharp pointed bills, are sure to be most formidable adversaries, who cruelly and completely avenge the linnets. Turbulent and heedless, flying low and close to the ground, goldfinches are easily inveigled into the snares that men, and especially children, set for them. Beware! then comes the cage and the humiliating labour of captivity!

The brilliant plumage of the goldfinch makes him a precious prey for bird-catchers. Proud of his fine appearance, and having the tastes of a high liver, he ends his career like those pretty fellows who exchange their beauty and poverty for the servitude of a rich marriage. When it is once shut up in its cage, the goldfinch will always find its table spread with an abundant supply of millet and hempseed, but it has to pay for this delicate fare by servile manœuvres. It is taught to fire a gun and to feign death; it is obliged to bear straps and to carry small pails of water for filling its bath.

But these are only some of the steps on the road to slavery, the first, the easiest to climb. Not only is the brilliant goldfinch obliged to earn his dinner by hard labour, but he is obliged to degrade himself by making love to a chattering, intemperate canary-hen. He becomes the father of mongrels, called canary-goldfinches, whose hybrid plumage is odious to his sight. Then, as a last mortification, the regimen of the prison tones down the colours and tarnishes that lustre of that brilliant garb of which he was so proud. His beautiful crimson mask takes an ugly sandy hue, and the bright golden spots on his wings grow dull. The beautiful, lively, merry bird grows coarse looking and vulgar, and if by chance a wild dapper goldfinch, proud of his freedom, passes near the cage where the poor prisoner is captive, he hardly recognises a friend and brother in the dull, coarse-looking, ill-mated bird, who has lost his golden spots behind his grating and who works like a galley-slave, piteous to behold, in the company of a jealous and peevish canary-hen.

THE LINNET AND THE SISKIN

On the crumbling walls of the orchard,
Where hangs the wealth of the broom,
He loves to sit in the scented breath
Of the apple trees in bloom.

He hides the pranks of his springtide love
And his nest with its chattering brood,
In the silent depths of an ancient wood,
Where he dwells in solitude.

Lost in the sky, o'er the branches high
Of even the topmost tree,
Singing so clearly, singing so merrily,
High in the air soars he!

THE LINNET AND THE SISKIN

Both these birds are great seed-eaters. Although their habits and origin are distinct, it is difficult to speak of them separately, for they resemble each other in many ways as regards disposition and mode of existence. They are both pleasing songsters, merry companions; their temper is docile and easy, and they can be tamed with facility. These amiable qualities are sure to make them more easily the prey of man, that false friend who loves birds only to put them into a cage in order to speculate on them.

The linnet, which is very common in our parts, is more

settled and homely in its habits than the siskin. In liberty in the woods its plumage is bright and pleasing. Its head and chest are of a fine red colour, its back is chestnut brown, its stomach reddish white, its wings and the feathers of its tail black, spotted with white. It is smaller in size than the goldfinch, and its bill is sharper. When it is shut up in a cage, like that bird it loses its liveliness and the oddness of its colours. The male, in a cage, soon gets to look like the female. The bright tints of its plumage fade insensibly; its garb turns brownish grey spotted with rusty dots — a vulgar and sad livery of bondage.

These birds chose their mates and build their nest in May. In wine countries they often build their nest among the vines on the vinepoles; in the neighbourhood of forests they choose thickets of young fir trees, and when one crosses such a wood in the time of pairing, one is sure to hear on all sides the song of linnets that are busily suspending their delicate dwellings on to the boughs of fir trees. The nest consists of small leaves, roots and moss on the outside, inside of feathers, hair and plenty of wool. On this soft bed the female lays six bluish white eggs, spotted with nut-brown at the broader end. When the young are grown enough to take their flight the whole houseful takes wing together; the whole clan of linnets congregates and starts off to explore the orchards and groves of the neighbourhood.

In spite of the approach of the bad season the flock does not separate. All winter long the numerous families of linnets continue to live sociably. They glean some scattered thistle-seed along the by-paths, perching on poplars and lime trees, picking the young buds; you can hear them twittering in the boughs as soon as the February sun sends some warm beams through the winter fogs. The males only are fine musicians. They begin with a light prelude which however is original only with wild linnets. The captive birds repeat only those strains that have been drilled into them; they are artists of inferior quality.

M. Gueneau de Montbeillard remarks a little sententiously that this is quite natural. « The bird whose voice has been formed in liberty, following only inner emotions, must have more touching accents than that which sings without an aim, only to kill time or to exercise its organs ».

The truth is that the art of song does not develop itself spontaneously even in singing-birds, but only by education and imitation. In the free state the young linnet forms its voice by hearing its father and other males of the neighbourhood repeat the old traditional melodies, which have been transmitted from one generation to another. The linnets that are born in a cage, or in the nest prepared by a bird-catcher, have often no other instructor than some boor who whistles some popular song for their benefit. These music lessons generally take place in the evening. Sometimes the bird-catcher, in order to excite the linnets to sing, takes them on his finger and holds them up in front of a mirror, where they imagine seeing a bird of their own species. While the master is whistling his ditty, they think that they hear their unknown companion; this illusion makes them giddy, and finally they all join in the chorus. It is a sad song of captivity without savour or perfume, and is no more like the pretty song of the wild linnet than the sickly lily of the valley raised in a hothouse can be compared to the vigorous balmy lily of the woods!

One would think that the slim and lively siskin with its olive-green plumage tinted with lemon colour, born in liberty and fond of long travels, would have a more independent character than the linnet. But this is a mere illusion. The siskin is like certain gypsies whose vagrant tastes do not exclude a certain fondness for servility. Although it bears a slight resemblance to the titmouse on account of its skill in climbing and in picking seed, yet it has not the undisciplined disposition of that valiant little bird.

It is said that in the free state they build their nests on the islands of the Rhine, in the Vosges mountains, in Hungaria, especially in woody, mountainous regions; but it is very difficult to find these nests. The birds hide them so skilfully in a litter of verdure, that they are said

LINNETS

to render them invisible by depositing in them a magic stone. They hide when they are pairing; their wooing is carried on mysteriously, so that nothing precise is known about the laying of their eggs. Being birds of passage, they come to our country at harvest time and select for their dwelling the banks of a river where alder trees grow, being very fond of that seed. As soon as cold weather sets in, they emigrate and do not return to France until orchards are in full bloom; they are particularly fond of apple tree blossoms.

The flight of the siskin is rapid and high; but it is as impetuous and simple minded as the linnet, and is easily caught in the grossest snares. A cage containing a captive siskin, serves as a decoy-bird; some lime-twigs set into the soil are sufficient to attract the giddy unsuspicious wayfarer. Then adieu to freedom; he will never see again the Vosges of Lorraine, nor his mysterious retreat in the heart of some fresh, green alder-grove.

In the aviary he will meet some other seed-eating birds, such as linnets and goldfinches, and like them, he will have to submit to the apprenticeship of bondage. Luckily his natural disposition is as docile as theirs and he gets easily accustomed to his new existence. Being provided with board and lodging, fresh water in his trough, and plenty of seed in his manger, he cares little about the rest. After a short time he will no longer regret the joyous vagrancy of open air life.

He even forgets to make love and if perchance he pairs with a canary, the ill-matched marriage generally remains barren, and the eggs when hatched are found to be empty. The siskin loses its faculty of reproduction in bondage, and also like the linnet and the goldfinch its bright tinted plumage.

THE GOLDHAMMER

June is the month of love, of a truth,
If a red is the colour of love and youth;
Strawberries glow in the burning noon,
And roses are red in the garden, in June.

Sunsets are red in the skies at night;
Clover in meadows is crimson bright;
Poppies also, like flames are seen,
Set in the wheat, so cool and green.

Pinks are red in the garden neat,
Cherries in orchards are red and sweet;
And there in the orchard, a thief is fed,
On ripe sweet cherries, both white and red.

Clear in the hush of the noontide heat,
The song of the goldhammer rises sweet.
A thankless churl must the farmer be,
Who'll grudge him a meal from the cherry-tree.

THE GOLDHAMMER

It was about Midsummer in the province of Poitou, at the time of mowing hay, when lime trees are covered with thousands of sweet-scented flowers and cherries are ripe. I was walking in a very productive orchard with a pretty girl, the niece of the owner of the property. The garden was green, full of cherry and other fruit-trees, all laden with fruit and situated near a wood full of birds.

My companion was a lovely girl of twenty, my own age; her complexion was rosy, her lips cherry-red; she was slender, delicately built, with beautiful black eyes and nut-brown hair. I had made her acquaintance only the day before, but in the country and especially in July, one grows soon intimate. The fresh morning-air, the bright sunshine, the delicious scent of new mown hay which came from the meadows set us yet more at ease, and we were walking under the trees in the garden chattering like a couple of old friends. She was of a merry disposition, very inquisitive and talkative; I rather timid and of a more romantic mood, easily inflamed and concealing under very awkward manners a latent tenderness which only demanded an opportunity to show itself more openly.

While we were loitering about, the song of a bird in the bowers struck our ear — a song consisting of short phrases, but of an exquisitely mellow sound. We could only compare it to the notes of a golden flute. It was a pure and full sound, wavering and yet tender at the same time.

The young girl stopped to listen.

« What bird is that singing so prettily? » asked she.

« It is a goldhammer. »

« Really, what is it like? I have never seen one. »

She made me describe to her the bird that was so fond of cherries. I tried to picture its beautiful yellow breast with its black wings; its half black and half yellow tail. I tried to give her an idea of the goldhammer, with its broad, wide open, purple-hued bill, its open nostrils, its large, round, dewy eye, red as a heart-cherry and moist as if it were bathed in dew, bewitching and irresistible; its slight black mustachio which gave such a *piquant* expression to its epicurian face. I told my companion that these birds come to us in the season when red and white heart-cherries take colour, and that they build their nest in the place where the highest boughs branch off. They line their nests delicately with soft grass and spider-webs, they suspend them like a hammock between two boughs by some supple but firm ligatures which swing the nest to and fro at the slightest breeze, thus adding a yet more voluptuous pleasure to the comfort of their aerial dwelling.

« Cherry-juice predisposes to tenderness » I continued, « and when the goldhammer has got drunk on wild cherries and on heart-cherries, he makes love to his sweetheart in his softly swinging nest. »

My pretty companion laughed at this remark and said that she should very much like to see a goldhammer.

I replied that it is not an easy matter, for the greedy bird has a very distrustful disposition and is rather unapproachable. I told her however that we might try.

We walked very stealthily hand in hand over the thick grass, taking great precaution not to startle the bird in the cherry-tree, and we drew near the large tree from which the melodious, flute-like notes issued. We had hardly reached the foot of the tree when the shy wild bird took wing, but we managed to perceive between the leaves its slender, well built body and its black and yellow wings, which were fluttering as it took its flight towards the wood.

We had remained some time near the cherry-tree, stretching our necks, hand in hand, raising our eyes to the bowers above us where the ripe fruit was shining between the leaves. They were red and white heart-cherries with fleshy pulp and inviting colour. A ladder just happened to be standing against the tree.

« Let us go and take the place of the goldhammer », she suggested, letting go my hand.

Pulling her skirts together, she lightly ascended the steps of the ladder, and from the foot of the tree I could distinguish in the shade her small feet half hidden under her striped pink dress. Half-way up the ladder, she turned around and said with an arch smile :

« Well ! are you not coming ? »

Of course I wished to come, but I should never have dared to do so without being invited. I followed her however blushing, and we both soon found ourselves in the heart of the tree.

The position was very pleasant, although not very comfortable; at the slightest movement we made, her arm and her hair would touch my cheek, but she was laughing, while I was looking very much constrained

THE GOLDHAMMER

and very foolish. At last she caught hold of the trunk of the tree, swinging herself on one of the horizontal boughs, sat on it as if she were on horseback. I did the same thing, and then we were sitting near each other, softly rocked to and fro on the elastic and flexible bough; only I had no comfortable prop to lean against, as she had, or rather my only prop would have been her waist and shoulders, and I was too stupidly timid to make use of it.

How I then envied the lightness and dexterity of the cherry-eating goldhammer! That epicurian bird knows how to poise himself on a bough, and that unsteady position between earth and sky neither prevents him from satisfying his greediness nor from making love to his sweetheart. Even when the wind shakes the tree, he swings with the foliage and loses neither his appetite nor his presence of mind.

I could not say the same of myself and in spite of the tempting company of my pretty neighbour, I was ill at ease and more embarrassed than before. She did not seem to notice it and went on merrily picking the cherries within reach of her hand and lips.

« It is very pleasant up here, do'nt you think so, said she; we are like the goldhammer and his sweetheart in their swinging nest. »

Did she wish me to imitate the goldhammer yet more completely? I was too stupid to understand her; besides it was as much as I could do to keep myself poised on the branch; a few minutes after I made a false movement and fell stupidly down at the foot of the tree.

She burst out laughing — a short nervous laugh — and after having stuffed her pockets with cherries, she too came down.

I was furious at myself, and we took our way homewards in almost perfect silence, ill-humoured; while on the outskirts of the wood the goldhammer was whistling his song as if he were laughing at my silliness.

THE KING-FISHER

When midsummer sun burns fierce as flame
From dawn till eve in the sky,
Come down with me to the rocky vale
Where the river glides softly by
And under the shade of the willow trees
The fishes in quiet lie.

In the sleepy shadows that fringe the stream,
The horehound and woodbine spring,
And hid in the herbage green and cool,
There nestles a wondrous thing
That darts like a fairy arrow sped
On a green and azure wing.

His wing just ruffles the glossy wave
As he skims o'er the placid stream,
Behold him, splendid in dazzling blue,
Lit up by the noontide beam!
If he would but stay! but he vanishes,
As swift as a passing dream.

THE KING-FISHER

During hot July days, I often recall to my mind a certain wooded pass in the forest of Auberive, where the Aube, yet near its source, opens its way between steep crags under the shade of hazel-nut, ash trees, and beeches. The branches are inextricably interwoven above the little river, so that it is almost dark there in broad daylight. A phosphorescent light filters through the dense foliage, and on the black soil — slimy alluvia — those plants abound that are usually found in damp places; rows of purple willows stand close together on the banks; the woodbine dips the fine feathered sprigs of its flesh-coloured tufts into the current; almond-scented meadow-sweet perfumes the air, whilst the dark red fruit of the wild raspberry bushes gleam in the darkness.

I used to scramble into the pass by letting myself down an almost impracticable path, fit only for goats, creeping like a cat under bowers of entangled brambles. In the hot hours of the afternoon I used to delight in this solitude and freshness. The dark river was murmuring softly ; now and then, some small bright drops would rain down from the overhanging branches and ripple the surface of the water. It was there that I made the acquaintance of the king-fisher.

The one that haunted that peaceful retreat had probably built its nest in the neighbourhood, in the lurking hole of some fresh-water crab, for I often saw it shoot like an arrow over the current. It used to graze the water with a plaintive cry and then disappear suddenly. I had hardly time to admire its back and its greenish blue tail, its wings and head covered with turquoise-coloured spots, its fiery-red breast and chest. At first, my presence used to disturb the wild, shy bird; but after a while, my discreet and peaceful mood would make it more confident, and it would finally circulate under the bushes, without heeding me any more than if I had been the trunk of a tree. I would often perceive it in the green, dim twilight of the sleeping river, perched motionless on a hazel-nut bough overhanging the current, its colours gleaming in the shade like those of some strange jewel set with sapphires, rubies and emeralds.

There it would perch for hours, with fixed gaze and bent head, watching for the passage of some small fry. Suddenly it let itself drop straight down into the transparent water; then it would reappear with some minnow or stickle-back in its bill, flying towards its hidden nest. It happened sometimes that after having dipped several times, it reappeared with nothing in its bill; it would then fly up the current, uttering a low plaintive cry and disappear again in search of some nook more abounding in fish.

Why are river birds almost always sad? The heron, the curlew, the snipe are melancholy birds; even the white wag-tail, with its everlasting motion on the gravel backwards and forwards, looks like a heartsick creature. Is their sadness caused by the influence of their haunts? Large ponds bordered with willows and reeds, in which the wind whistles, morning and evening mists, the murmur of hidden forest springs, all these incite man to melancholy; do they act in the same manner on the nervous system of birds? One is inclined to believe so. However, for the king-fisher as well as for the heron, there is a more prosaic reason for their peevish disposition: the uncertainty of their daily subsistence, the anxiety with which these birds have to watch for their prey for hours at the same spot, are surely enough to account for it. When one's stomach is empty and one has to kick one's heels till some problematic fish comes into reach of one's bill, one is not inclined to be foolishly merry. Even those who follow this occupation for pleasure and are sure of finding a good supper when they come home, contract the habit of nervous melancholy in the long hours of watching. Nearly all anglers are predisposed to hypochondria.

The king-fisher spends its life in an often deceptive quest after food, in a painful struggle for existence. It has hardly time to think of love. Its nuptials are of very short duration; it builds its nest hastily, deposits six or seven white eggs, and as soon as the young are hatched it takes wing again in search of its daily subsistence. In the fine season, such a life is bearable, but when the winter is severe and streams are frozen, it is obliged to beat a long time along the banks of the river before it finds its prey, and more than once it drops down starved on the frozen river.

This wild and noble-looking bird is a restless rover, a lover of solitary strands and shady retreats; he looks like an exiled prince who has been changed into an animal by some evil fairy. The Greeks believed him to be Alcyone, the daughter of Eolus, that had been metamorphosed into a bird. In our own time the king-fisher is still the object of vague superstition in some rural districts. As the country-people

THE KINGFISHER

see it ordinarily posted on dead branches, they say that it dries up the wood on which it perches. In Buffon's time, people had noticed that worms rarely prey upon its dead body, and therefore good housewives attributed to it the virtue of keeping away moths, and used to suspend the dead bird in the midst of their woolen garments.

But everything is getting vulgar and mean, even superstitions. In losing its melodious name of Alcyon, the unlucky king-fisher has lost even that poetical halo which still shines after death.

Whilst I was giving myself up to these reflexions, the hot July afternoon was drawing to a close. The sun was already lower and shooting oblique beams under the arch formed by the beeches, and the rays were running over the black surface of the river, like some marvellous golden-hued insect. At the same time a breath of fresh air was shaking the leafy bowers, making here and there an opening for the light to pass, ruffling the surface of the rivulet with golden ripples. Then, little by little, the illusion would die away, and I could only see water spiders dancing a fantastic ballet on the placid waters.

The king-fisher would again shoot across the darkness like the fitful glimmer of a rainbow. **He would** turn ever and anon about the level of the current, like an experienced marauder who knows that the hours of twilight are more favourable for his sport. Then suddenly he would disappear under the water, reappear all dripping, carrying away some fish in his bill, whilst flying towards his nest. I would hear a concert of shrill pipings in the distance, issuing from the knotted roots on the banks of the river. It was thus that the birdlings were welcoming the return of the king-fisher and his booty.

THE SPARROW

Let skies be cloudy or skies be blue,
Little brown sparrow, away go you,
Ever in search of food or fun,
Come summer or winter, rain or sun.

Boughs of lilac whereon to rest
April spreads when you build your nest;
Autumn feeds you with golden corn,
And berries ripe on the wayside thorn.

Winter comes with its frost and snow;
Waters may freeze and winds may blow,
Yet little you reck, and nought you rue,
For every hand has a crumb for you.

Through sunshine to-morrow and storm to-day
You go, like a friar of orders gray,
Finding, wherever your fancy leads,
A table spread for the wanderer's needs.

THE SPARROW

The sparrow is like the lark a bird more particularly found in France. Whilst the lark represents certain lyrical sides of the French race, its dauntless buoyancy, its spirited liveliness, the sparrow, is the emblem of gallic petulancy, of the noisy, jolly animal spirits of the people of Paris. Therefore it is in Paris where one can best observe the habits of these sharp, impudent, pilfering birds of passage. They congregate in swarms on the roofs of Parisian houses, in the noisiest streets, in the most frequented gardens. Clad in a grey and brown costume, scarcely brightened up by a white and black tie round the throat and a yellowish line on the wings, the sparrow, with its vulgar manners, its monotonous, cry, makes no outside show; but it is one of these people that one must not judge by its clothes. It is like one of those ugly persons, who are bewitching when their features are in full play. The charm of the sparrow consists in the saucy liveliness of its hazel-nut coloured eye, in its skipping movements, in the play of its frolicsome countenance and the pretty wagging of its head.

In Paris sparrows are in their true medium. The Parisians are fond of them and they are fond of the Parisians, and the jolly, saucy bird is impregnated with all the faults and all the virtues of the population in the midst of which it lives familiarly. It loves the noisy, animated public roads; it is fond of crowds, and it has taken from the *Gamin de Paris,* the taste of loitering about the streets like a vagrant. It is not very domestic. Its brother, the tree sparrow, builds a regular nest on a tree; the Parisian sparrow, nestles rather at random, in the hole of some wall, in the gutter of a roof, or behind some window shutter. There, hastily, without any artistic rules it piles together all sorts of rags, bits of straw or hay, but only just what is necessary to build and line a nest. It does not loiter long in its dwelling. The noises of the street are too tempting to be resisted. Presto! As soon as the young ones are feathered, you can see them flying on the paving stones. It is not rare; in the Tuileries or Luxembourg gardens at the turning of some shady walk to meet a sparrow, the head of the family, the young ones trudging after the father, hopping and piping, and opening wide their large yellow bill for the father to feed.

Although the nest of the Parisian sparrow is far from comfortable, still it is rarely empty. As soon as one brood has moved out, another one takes its place. The female sparrow is remarkably prolific, and her progeniture can rival even that of Mother Goose's « Old Woman who lived in a Shoe. » From the beginning of May to the end of September each couple has hatched at least three broods. The rapid multiplication of these roguish birds is the despair of gardeners and cultivators. In Paris, where vine-arbours and fruit walls are rare, the pilfering disposition of the sparrows does not draw on them public reprobation; on the contrary, the population is rather prone to encourage and to develop it yet more. Hardly a Parisian exists who does not feed regularly a sparrow or two. The civil service officer, the clerk going to his office, the shop-girl on her way to her place of employment, stop on their way in the Tuileries to throw a handful of crumbs to some band of sparrows. Between eleven and twelve in the morning you can see on all window-sills many charitable hands preparing a meal for these happy and amiable vagrants.

Ye frisky, talkative sparrows! You are indeed the

spoiled guests of the great city, the cheerfulness and animation of the Parisian streets:

> Fearless, confident and bold
> Birds by thousands flying,
> Flapping every shining wing
> Fill the air with chattering,
> And with fledglings reared to rove
> Like themselves, o'er field and grove.
>
> Pilfering where'er they go
> What they choose for forage,
> Whatsoever farm or field
> Garden-plot or park may yield,
> Whether autumn reigns or spring,
> The winged nation thrive and sing!

"In the whole city their cover is laid and they know it well! They know where the best morsels are awaiting them and are sure to be there in time. It is marvelous to see the rapidity with which they communicate to one another the news of some extraordinary treat. An old gentleman was telling me that every morning after breakfast he was in the habit of distributing bread crumbs to about twenty sparrows. One day, having exhausted his stock of bread, he gave them cake instead. The sparrows, liked this change of fare and probably told their friends and acquaintances about the good luck that had befallen them; for the next day the old gentleman found that he had sixty guests instead of twenty.

THE SPARROW

> Qu'on aille soutenir, après un tel récit,
> Que les bêtes n'ont pas d'esprit

(Let it be said after this, that birds and beasts have no intelligence!)

In the fine season they put a cage on a balcony near my dwelling, in which some canaries are chirping from night to morning. As soon as their daily portion of millet and chickweed has been placed in their cage, the sparrows who have been watching the proceedings from the opposite roof, hasten up shrieking, and the brazen-faced creatures who know no fear, pick away the best of the millet and chickweed in spite of the indignant cries and protestations of the canaries, which only excite yet further the boldness of the marauders.

In summer, the life of the Parisian sparrow is a long holiday, an uninterrupted season of love making, of abundant, and choice dinners. But summer does not last forever. Gradually, autumn is approaching; the leaves of the chestnuts fall with the cool days of September. Sparrows, with their subtle scent, have a presentiment of short and rainy days, of long, cold nights, of snow-covered roofs, of muddy streets, closed windows, of scarcer, and less choice dinners. You can see them congregate on the large trees in squares and gardens, taking counsel together. Will winter be there soon? Will it be severe? Is it necessary to think seriously of leaving the country? Their instinct tells them that yonder, beyond the city gates, there are fields that have been freshly sown with good grain, and farms with well-stored granaries. The greediest, the least courageous birds decide to leave the country, and suddenly you can see flights of sparrows leaving the thin foliage of the trees to emigrate towards the plains of the provinces of Beauce and Brie.

But the true Parisian sparrows, those who love the big city even in its winter ugliness, do not leave it. Brave little creatures as they are, they set at defiance all the evil chances of the winter season, quarelling over stray bits of food under the very hoofs of the horses; finally they go and rap with their bill against the familiar windows which just open to throw some crumbs to these faithful friends of good and evil days.

THE WATER WAG-TAIL

Timidly and soberly dight
In feathers of black and white
We find you hopping away
    Pert, brisk and gay.

Women come clattering here
To wash in the river so clear;
Yet, pert little Wagtail, you dare
To stay; for the noisy folk there
    Little you care.

You love to mock urchins who think
To catch you, and just on the brink
Of the river you stand and you stay
Till they hear you; then, off and away!
    Brisk, pert and gay!

THE WAG-TAIL

Under this generic name people often confound the ordinary wag-tail and the dishwasher. The habits and costume of these two birds are however very different. The plumage of the wag-tail is yellow with an olive brown tint; it dwells in prairies where cattle comes to graze, or it flutters about in the fields following the labourers; the dish-washer on the contrary is clothed in black and white and prefers to frequent shallow rivulets or the banks of rivers. They have in common certain particular traits of face and gait: both have a fine bill, thin, long feet, a long tail which they are incessantly wagging, whence the French name of « hoche-queue » (wag-tail) given to them in the province of Lorraine. They are great devourers of flies and gnats; but the dish-washer prefers river-flies, whereas the wag-tail has a weakness for large blue-bottle flies.

The dish-washer is a friend of strands and damp river banks; it likes to haunt mill-dams and the neighbourhood of washing-places. Neither the noise of the mill-wheel, spluttering about its drops of white foam, nor the noise of the washerwomen agitating their beetles, can frighten them. They trip with quick, nimble tread over stones and gravel; they dip their feet into the water and are perpetually wagging their long white and black tails, as if they were trying to imitate the motion of the beetles on the linen.

These birds emigrate in winter and do not return till the end of March. They build their nest on the ground near hollow river banks, or under stakes of wood built up near the river. Their nest consists of dried grasses and small roots, lined on the inside with feathers and hair; the female wag-tail lays four or five white eggs, covered with brown spots. She is a very good mother, very proud of the neatness of her dwelling, which she keeps most scrupulously clean like a very careful housekeeper.

When the birdlings are able to fly, the father and

mother take them along the banks of rivulets and keep watch over them for about a month longer. Quite recently, on the banks of lake Annecy in Savoy. I witnessed the restless uneasiness and agitation of a couple of wag-tails, one of whose fledglings had got astray under a garret-window and was not able to get out again. Not only the wag-tails chaperon their children, but they teach them to catch flies whilst they are taking their flight. You can see them then rising by starts. turning round and round, wheeling about by means of their tail which they spread out like a fan ; whilst they are fluttering, they utter a low, sharp, shrill, redoubled cry, having a clear, distinct sound.

The dish-washer is a very nervous bird, its vivacity is almost restlessness. It appears to be very familiar, and yet it is very difficult to catch. As soon as you approach. it will fly away ten steps further, perch somewhere else wagging its tail, as if it were setting the person who is pursuing it at defiance; then again it will take its flight, and these proceedings go on for hours. One of my friends, a poet, has tried to characterize in a few verses the nervous, deceiving flight of the dish-washer :

> Elle semble, la belle,
> Un maitre de chapelle
> Blanc et noir.
> Qui rythme la cadence
> Du moulin et la danse
> Du battoir.

> Elle court sur le sable
> Elle s'envole, semblable
>   Au désir
> Qui toujours nous devance
> Et qui fuit dès qu'on pense
>   Le saisir...

(« Like a capel-master, the beautiful bird, in black and white garb, seems to be marking the rythm of the mill and the motion of the beetles of the washerwomen.

It runs on the gravel, it takes its flight onward and upward; like our wishes, it flies off as soon as we hope to seize it. »)

The grey and yellow wag-tails have more pastoral habits. « The wag-tail, which lives on flies, » says old Belon, « loves to follow cattle, knowing that it will find food, and it is perhaps for that reason that we have called it « Bergerette » (Shepherdess). It is more sedentary in its tastes than the dish-washer and does not leave us even in the bad season. In winter, it gets nearer to villages, seeks shelter near the banks of ponds which freeze only rarely, and there, in spite of cold, it sings a low, soft, discreet strain. As soon as the month of March brings back the season of field labour and sowing, you can see the wag-tail following the labourer who is pushing his plough, or perching on mounds of fresh soil where it is sure to find an ample provision of worms.

In April it begins to build its nest in the fields or sometimes in the roots of some tree on the banks of a

THE WAGTAIL

rivulet. The nest, placed on the ground, is very much like that of the dish-washer, as far as choice of materials and texture is concerned, only it is interwoven more carefully. The female lays six or seven eggs; they are of a whitish hue with yellowish spots. When the young ones are fledged, towards mowing-time, the father and mother take them to some new-mown fields where the cattle are taken to pasture.

Then begins an idyllic life for the wag-tail. The big, russet-coloured oxen are lying about on the short grass of the pasture-commons; around them, swarms of flies are buzzing, and to the right and left bands of long-tailed birds dart on the insects, without being in the least frightened by the neighbourhood of the weighty ruminants. Some of the wag-tails are daring enough to perch on the black horns of the cows. Others follow the sheep dispersed about the commons, following the lead of the shepherd, who walks ahead, wrapped in his cloak.

In the XVIII. century, when naturalists yet lent to the animals they were studying the sentimental ideas that were then the fashion, they pretended that wag-tails were so fond of the shepherd as to warn him when a wolf or a sparrow-hawk was drawing near. This story is as ingenious and pretty as it is unlikely. Wag-tails care little about the wolf of whom they have nothing to fear; as to the hawk, they are very much agitated when they see it soaring above the pasture-commons, it is therefore only interest for their own preservation and not friendship for the shepherd who does not fear that bird, which causes their warning, for a hawk will attack birds but never flocks of sheep.

All day long the wag-tail will follow the herds in their evolution. Now, evening draws near : the shadows of the elms lengthen on the plains; light mists arise in the back ground; the moon shows her crescent above the dusky woods; the shepherd is blowing his horn to call his scattered sheep; pushed by the dogs, the flocks rush forward on the dusty road, bleating noisily, the bellowing cows turn their heads towards their stable, and in the rear, hopping over tufts of grass, wagging their tail and uttering low, shrill cries, the wag-tails accompany the herd to the extremity of the fields.

THE STONE-CHAT

Look you how, struggling through a watery sky,
The autumn sun shines faintly on the lea,
Full gently fall, on soft green moss to lie,
Leaves, dropping one by one from every tree.

O'er all the misty hollows of the plain
And moorland wide, how deep a quiet broods!
Only the faint, low music of the rain,
Breaks the sweet silence of these solitudes.

See how the shower has hung with limpid pearls
Each bush and thorn and spike of lovely blue!
Anon there comes a sudden gust and whirls
The gathered treasure down, in drops of dew.

Hark! yon red throated stone-chat hopping near
Trills forth a sudden warble loud and long;
Bird of the lonely waste, how sweet and clear,
Loved by the listening shepherd, is thy song!

THE STONE-CHAT

I had been visiting the museum of Saint-Malo. As I was walking along the well-lighted rooms, where you can see through the windows the blue sea, I stopped at a showcase containing a large collection of birds belonging to that region, such as warblers, titmice, nightingales, blue-breasts, red-breasts, etc. Near the white-tail, I saw another small bird, with a red breast and a black head marked with two white spots on each side of the neck; the back was black also, shaded off with brown, just like the tail; the wings of the same black colour, were delicately marked with a white line.

I recognized the stone-chat, which they call the *hammerer* in my province, and the description that old Belon has given of it recurred to my mind : « You can see it perching on the highest tree-tops, constantly flapping its wings, on account of this unceasing restlessness they call it *traquet* or mill-clapper; for as the mill-clapper never stops, as long as the mill-stone is grinding, so this restless bird is for ever flapping its wings. »

Satisfied with having seen the stone-chat again, I left the museum, recalling to my mind the pretty countenance of that lover of bushy moors. I crossed the narrow streets of Saint-Malo, lined on each side with tall houses, and I was drawing near the sunshiny quays, where I could see the outlines of multitudes of masts, clearly defined on the surface of the greenish white sea. The wind had risen, the boats were dancing along the slips, and I could perceive beyond the wall of the quay the tops of their masts rocking to and fro. On the opposite side of the bay, Dinard was spreading out in the sun its terrace-like gardens and its Italian villas. The boats were now leaving the slips and taking advantage of the wind to sail towards the river Rance. The steam ferry boat, filled with passengers, was slowly crossing the bay, leaving behind it a long wake of white foam. The animation which seemed to reign on the water and in the air induced me to take a trip also ; so I jumped into a boat, and told them to take me to the Point of *Vicomté*. There, I climbed up the woody slope and found myself soon in the middle of a large moor.

The pasture-commons were bordered by thick hedges of brambles and woodbine; these commons stretch to a long distance, separated here and there by some rather barren fields, where, nevertheless, a meagre crop of golden corn and light yellow oats was growing, marking light spots on the vast extent of the moor. I was turning my back to the bay which was hidden from my view by a wood of beeches, but I could hear the low, rythmical rising and heaving of the sea. On a holly-covered hill, a shepherd was watching his russet-brown cows buried up to their knees in the greyish verdure of the furze. A profound silence, a great calm was reigning all around; even the light seemed to be toned down, the sun being veiled by white clouds. Suddenly, I heard a low cry repeated several times: Ouip! tiay! tiay! Ouip! tiay, tiay! And a few steps off, swinging contentedly on a bit of woodbine, I perceived my birdling of the museum, with its russet-brown breast, the stone-chat of the shepherds.

Perched on its unsteady stem, already impatient to take its flight, it flew by short starts towards another branch, where it would remain a few minutes and then leave again for some other bough. It represented perpetual motion. Although it never soared high, its black feet never seemed to touch the branches, and they seem to belong rather to the air than to the ground. While the stone-chat was continually dancing on the flexible stems of the brambles and woodbine, it seemed to be perfectly happy, uttering now and again its low cry: Ouip! tiay, tiay! Ouip! tiay, tiay!

The stone-chat builds its nest in waste land, among the roots of entangled bushes; it hides its nest carefully and enters it stealthily, like a lover who fears to be seen when he visits his mistress. The female lays five or six eggs of a bluish green colour, with slight russet-coloured spots near the broader end. As soon as the young ones are hatched, the stone-chat takes great care not to be seen entering or leaving its nest. It never dares to go near it without having made its way through the neighbouring bushes, so as to render the search of ill-intentioned people entirely fruitless, at least as much as lies in its power. When it leaves its nest, it takes the same precautions as on entering it; it glides under the branches till it gets to a certain distance, so that one never knows the exact place of its nesting, and it is necessary to search along the whole hedge to be able to discover any trace of it.

People who are so exceedingly mistrustful are rarely of a very sociable disposition. Except in pairing-time, the stone-chat lives in solitary retirement. « It does not fly in company with others; it is always alone, » says Belon; « nevertheless, in the fields it is easily approached, and only flies to short distances, without appearing to take any notice of the hunter. »

THE STONE-CHAT

The stone-chat that I had been following on the moor of *Vicomté* did not seem in the least to pay any attention to my presence. It continued to hop over the furze and the holly, chirping and fluttering all the time. It took me thus a long distance, stopping now and then as if it were waiting for me, and then starting off again as soon as I got up to it. Above, the white and blue marbled sky was shedding a soft light over the moor. Beyond the pasture-commons, above the foliation of the bushes which bent back and seemed to have been clipped by the seawind as by a hedge-bill, I could perceive the bluish waters of the Rance; and on the opposite shore, the slate-covered cupola of the church of Saint-Servan, the tower of Solidor, the white villas of Dinard, embowered in verdure; then, behind a rocky point, the elegant spire of Saint-Malo; lastly, quite in the background, the foamy sea, dotted with brown rocks, on which innumerable sails were flying. I was yet listening to the small, solitary bird humming its short song in this immensity, and I felt a sensation of serene joyousness in the presence of these silent spaces of sky, earth, and air, animated only by the dull chirping of this small creature, at once so wild and so familiar. I envied its vivacity and sprightliness. I watched it as it fluttered above the furze, where the cows were still grazing, half hidden in the verdure. Everything seemed to be living and breathing with the placid unconcern of creatures and inanimate things that are sure of seeing again, on the morrow, the spectacle that they saw the day before; moving slowly in the same circle of pleasant, monotonous occupations.

Suddenly, the stone-chat took a quicker, longer flight towards the river; I could distinguish it like a black spot on the surface of the blue water; then I lost sight of it and remained alone on the green moor facing the sea, now rising with a murmur as soft and as low as a nurse's lullaby.

THE NUT-HATCH

Come into the depths of the forest,
  Alone, alone with me,
Under the sweet and swaying boughs
  Of the bonied linden-tree.

Far and wide the green trees wave,
  Like waters wide and free;
Meseems we look up to the lofty sun
  Through depths of the clear green sea.

Tac, tac, tac, tac!... In the stillness
  How weird those accents seem!
They hold us silent and spell-bound
  Entranced in a woodland dream.

Is it a wood-nymph pining
  In the heart of her hollow tree?
Rending the woods with her fairy hand
  Because she would fain be free?

Tac, tac, tac, tac! 'T is a *Nut-hatch*!
  Hunting for grubs is he!
How he digs, and digs, and hammers away
  Up in that old oak tree!

THE NUT-HATCH

AND THE LESSER WOOD-PECKER

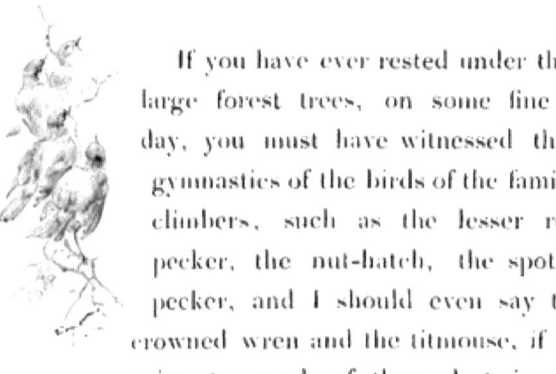

If you have ever rested under the shade of large forest trees, on some fine summer's day, you must have witnessed the amusing gymnastics of the birds of the family of small climbers, such as the lesser red wood-pecker, the nut-hatch, the spotted wood-pecker, and I should even say the golden crowned wren and the titmouse, if I were not going to speak of these last in a separate chapter. In the distance, in the solemn silence of the big forest, you can hear the shrill cry and picking of the large climbers: the green wood-pecker, the great black nut-hatch and the lesser wood-pecker. The small people of this family make less noise, but accomplish perhaps more. They only utter now and then low cries of appeal, running along the branches and destroying numberless caterpillars, larvae and eggs of various insects.

The lesser red wood-pecker has the brightest colours. Its spotted black and white plumage is set off by a pure red spot on the top of its head. It is hardly of the size of a sparrow. Like the large witwall, it has all the distinctive traits of the boldest climbers : a hard bill, a long and moveable back nail; its tail feathers are rugged and strong enough to be used as a prop, when the bird, hanging with its back downward, redoubles the clatter of its bill against the boughs. It does not climb very high, but circulates around the trunk of trees with marvelous agility. In the fine season it builds its nest in rotten trees where dampness has made holes in the boughs; it often has to fight for these lodgings with the great black-headed titmouse; this latter bird, however, not being so strong as the woodpecker with its sharp bill and nails, is obliged to leave the field of battle. Like the great wood-pecker, the female lesser red wood-pecker lays three white eggs in this rudimentary nest, which she patiently hatches on a bed of wood-dust. These birds do not emigrate. In winter they keep near habitations and like to frequent orchards, where they carefully pick all the fruit-trees they can find. This ferreting and picking propensity develops prudence and ingeniousness in the wood-pecker. Its disposition is cunning and distrustful. It is difficult to perceive this bird in the woods; as soon as it has the presentiment that a stranger is approaching, it remains motionless behind the trunk of a tree, and you can scarcely perceive a bit of its head, in which an arch eye is glistening. When it is going to take a drink, it flies up to the pond very slowly, by starts, and silently. Then it descends from tree to tree, until it reaches the water, turning its head every minute, like a thief who has been pilfering and is afraid of being caught.

The nut-hatch has often been confounded with the group of wood-peckers, but it differs from them in many respects. In Lorraine they call the nut-hatch « Pic maçon », and in some other provinces « Pic bleu » (blue woodpecker). It has their strong bill, but its tail is not so stiff; its own tail is moveable like that of the white wag-tail; this latter circumstance makes the gait of the nut-hatch much more elegant and supple than that of the wood-peckers. It is of the same size as the lesser red wood-pecker and its feet are like those of the last-named birds provided with hooked nails. The head, back and tail of the male nut-hatch are of a fine ash-blue colour; its throat and cheeks are whitish; its breast and stomach orange coloured; its wings brown with dark grey edges. Its bill is awl-shaped, rounded off at the end, straight and resisting like forged steel, for this reason the nut-hatch can hammer and pick the bark of trees, making a great noise, and when it holds a nut, it pierces the fruit easily; thence its English name of nut-hatch.

It runs over the boughs of trees in every direction, hanging often with its head downward, in search of caterpillars and small grub. It choses its dwelling ordinarily in the depths of the forest where it leads a most industrious, solitary life. It is a silent bird. The only cry it utters when pursuing insects is a soft murmur: ti! ti! ti! Sometimes it introduces its bill into the bark of a tree, making a peculiar, loud, jarring noise, as if it wished to frighten the prey it is pursuing, and to take advantage of its disarray to surprise it more easily. In spring, the male nut-hatch has a peculiar cry like a roll-call: guirie! guirie! it repeats this cry constantly when calling its sweet-heart.

As soon as pairing has taken place, the husband and wife both busily arrange the nest, which they have built in the holes of a tree. If the opening is too large, they build it up with mud, leaving only sufficient room for their own egress and ingress; they consolidate this masonry yet more by mixing some pebbles with mud, and that is why this bird in France is often called « Pic maçon ». In this obscure nest the female lays five or six greyish eggs, with russet coloured spots. It hatches them assiduously, whilst the male goes to look for food. The young ones are hatched in May, and as soon as they are strong enough to seek their own subsistence, the family separates. « Peasants have observed, » says the naturalist Belon, « that the male

THE NUT-HATCH

bird beats the female when he finds her after she has left him. There is a proverb about people who live happily together in matrimony, that they resemble the nut-hatch ». From this we can conclude than in the opinion of the old naturalist the happiest matches would be those where the wife likes to be beaten.

Be this as it may, family life among the nut-hatches does not seem to be of long duration after the young ones are hatched. When autumn draws nigh, each male takes its own way. Sometimes they meet later in the season under hazel-nut trees; they do not recognize each other but pick and quarrel over some fresh kernel.

The lesser spotted wood-pecker is yet smaller than the nut-hatch; it is nearly of the same size as the wren and has the extreme agility of that little bird. Its plumage is grey and russet coloured; its throat is pure white and its head has a brownish tinge. It dwells the whole year where it was born, in holes of trees; there it establishes its brood and spends its days picking at moss in the cleft bark of trees. It runs over the boughs so rapidly that it is often confounded with the troglodyte. It is marvelously skilful in gymnastics, and a most ingenious destroyer of caterpillars; it ought to be venerated by all those who are fond of sylviculture. It inspects the trees, branch after branch, living on the leaf-covered stems, exploring them head downwards, or in every other imaginable position. On and under the leaves, in every chink or cleft of the boughs, it finds thus the grub and flies which constitute its food.

All these lesser climbers have quick movements and a low discreet voice; they are the life of thickets and large forests, where singing birds seldom penetrate. They animate the depths of the great woods. Their light, easy movements harmonize with the creaking of boughs and branches, the rustling of leaves, the murmur of springs in the moss, the dull humming of insects, and all those thousand minute voices of the forest, which apparently silent, are yet never quite dumb.

THE LARK

O thou sweet songster of the summer sky,
How joyous is the Song, that from on high
Thou pourest down, to glad the listening wold,
O lark! sweet songster of the summer sky!

Straight as an arrow speeding to its mark
Up to the noonday sun thou soars't sweet lark,
Leaving the mists below thee, grey and cold
    Thou the sweet songster of the summer sky!

High in the blue, still as a floating cloud,
Hovering o'er earth's wide pastures, sweet and long
Thou singest; and all the azure heaven is loud
With the resounding music of thy song
    O lark! sweet songster of the summer sky!

THE LARK

When I was twenty years old and living in a country town, several friends and I hired a small place near the town; it had a garden where we had the intention of studying practical horticulture seriously. We used to meet there early in the morning on fine summer days, and we set to digging, watering plants and weeding, thus spending in physical labour the fulness of our exuberant, youthful days. Sometimes we would spend the whole day in the woods and sit down to dine in excellent appetite, after having roasted a leg of mutton as well as we could in the open air.

One evening, I decided on spending the whole night in the same quarters and I settled myself comfortably in a hammock, suspended on the cross-beams of the thatched roof of our rustic dining-room. I fell asleep about eleven o'clock. The night was deliciously warm, embalmed by the scent of pines; across the murmuring branches my sleepy eyes could yet distinguish the golden stars twinkling in the sky above my head; my sleeping-chamber was exceedingly comfortable and I slept soundly all night through, until the first faint glimmer of dawn. The freshness which always falls in woods at sunrise having awaked me, I jumped out of my hammock and began to walk about, so as to restore suppleness to my benumbed members.

The coppice was yet silent. Fine drops of pearly dew were hanging on the leaves and the blades of grass, so that the gossamer threads between the brambles seemed to be covered with diamonds. When I reached the extremity of the wood, I was suddenly cheered by a joyous strain which seemed to drop from the pearl-gray sky. On the whole extent of the plain which lay waving before me, hundreds of larks were taking their flight from among the barley and oat fields, rising in short windings and soaring upwards towards the blue, slightly shaded sky. I could see their small brown bodies rising whilst they were fluttering in their aerial ascension; then suddenly they twinkled in a ray of sunshine and I lost sight of them in the heights of the blue heavens.

I could no longer distinguish them, but their strain, with its merry, crystalline notes was still resounding in the air. You would have thought that the blue space above had suddenly become melodious and was singing that lovely song. Now and then a lark would drop down from the heights of the clouds, straight as a plumb-line; within one foot from the soil, it would make a winding so as to crouch in some furrow. Another lark would then soar upwards twittering, and all along, from the gray plain to the luminous sky above, there was a constant forward and backward motion of sonorous voices and fluttering wings.

Never had a bird's song given me a fresher and a more delicious sensation than this charming serenade at dawn, and ever since that delightful morning in the woods, I began to love larks.

These birds are untiring musicians. Other birds sing but two months in the year in spring; but larks never tire of charming the aerial spaces. From early April to October they never cease their joyous strain. On the ground they are mute, but as soon as they begin to wing their flight upwards, they become melodious. The higher they soar, the more strength their voice acquires. They seem to be animated and inspired by light. It is not only love that develops their voice, as it is with other singing birds; they continue their song long after the broods are hatched, till the latter end of autumn. Guesneau de Montbeliard thinks that larks sing so long only to sustain each other, and to persuade themselves that they are strong enough to keep birds of prey at a distance. This explanation is very ingenious, but it does not quite satisfy me. Of course I am aware that children and cowards are in the habit of singing when they are crossing a wood at nightfall, to give themselves courage. In spite of this, I have too great a faith in the intelligence of larks to believe them capable of making use of such a childish proceeding. To sing as loud as one can, even in company, does not appear to me to be a very practical means of diverting the attention of gerfalcons and sparrow-hawks. I prefer believing that the open air and the sunlight exhilarate the larks and thus develop their musical powers exceedingly. Generally the male sings loudest and best, so as to attract the attention of the female; when he has discovered the one he was seeking, he dashes down precipitously and pairs with her.

As soon as courtship and pairing are over, the female builds her nest between two clods of soil and lines it inside with dry grasses. She lays four or five spotted eggs, brown or gray, which she hatches hastily. As soon as the young ones are feathered, they leave their nest and roam about the fields under the lead of the mother, and this promptness often misleads those who are hunting for bird's nests.

The readiness with which young larks leave their nest

THE LARK

after they are hatched, has not escaped the attention of the fabulist La Fontaine. Much has been said to disparage his sense of observation, but notwithstanding this he was a close observer of the things of nature. In the well-known fable : « The Lark and her young », he has remained faithful to truth when he speaks of the rapidity with which the mother « lays her eggs, broods and hatches them hastily », and the firmness with which the mother commands her young ones « to march off in silence » as soon as the owner of the field has declared his last intentions to his son, is justified by a close observation of the habits of larks and the system of education applied to their young.

Whilst these are tripping over the stubble fields, the mother keeps flying about them with constant care and solicitude. She feeds them with worms, caterpillars, ant's eggs and grasshoppers. This however is only the food of their infancy, for as soon as they are grown, they become granivorous and seek their subsistence in vegetable food. In summer, during courtship and pairing, the season of song and of bold soaring upwards, larks are very lean ; but they make up for lost time towards autumn, when they live more on the ground ; eating at all hours, they then grow plump and fat.

Then comes the critical moment of their existence ; man begins to hunt and to decimate them. He hunts them in every imaginable way, with nets, with a mirror ; he uses every means to destroy these charming birds ; although they render such marked service to agriculture by devouring all kinds of injurious insects. It is true that hunters pretend that they also devour grain, but this accusation is but a stupid pretext for roasting pitilessly thousands of these small birds on a spit. If there is no stop put to this, the whole species will soon be destroyed, and then the joyous strain of the skylark will no longer resound in the air. The pitiless peasant will be astonished at the silence of the plain; he will regret the merry little bird whose joyous song charmed his rude labour of ploughing and sowing.

THE RED-START

In the porch of an empty cottage,
In a hole in the granite wall,
Is the place that the Redstart chooses
For his nest so soft and small.

On the crumbling walls of a ruin,
Where wallflowers bloom in the spring,
It is safe, in the quiet woodlands,
To open his heart and sing.

He knows that mankind are traitors,
And foes to birds of the air,
And in depths of the briars and brushwood
He hides from the fowler's snare.

THE RED-START

AND THE BLUE-BREAST

 Although these two birds differ in colour, they have nevertheless more than one point in common: they are both fine singers, with delicate bills and voluble throats and a soft, lovely eye; both are fond of solitude, flying from noise and loving intimacy; they come to us in spring and emigrate in autumn.

The red-start, which is called red-wing in some countries, is smaller in size than its cousin the nightingale; its throat and neck are brown, as well as the line round its eyes; a brown frontlet covers its forehead; the top of the head and its back are dark grey, the breast of a fine russet red, and this bright hue is repeated on the whole extent of its tail feathers, excepting the two middle ones which are brown. But all these tints are much less marked and much toned down in the female red-start.

These birds are especially to be found in mountainous regions; they prefer to settle down in abandoned huts or on the roofs of empty dwellings. Ruins attract them; they harmonize with the wild, untamed disposition of the red-start. There they find ivy-covered walls, tufts of wall-flowers, entangled brambles and briers, under all of which they can build their nest in peace. Very often, in the neighbourhood of lake Annecy, in Savoy, whilst I was climbing the steep, rocky ascent which leads to the *Tournettes*, I frightened some couples of red-starts, who thought they were quite hidden in safety in these solitary pine forests, where no other noise is to be heard but the foaming of mountain torrents, and in the far distance, the feeble, silvery tinkling of the *clarin* or cow-bells, which recall the herds of cattle scattered in the pasture.

The female red-start lays five or six bluish eggs. These birds are naturally of a very mistrustful disposition. It is said that they abandon their nest as soon as they perceive that they are watched in the process of nest-building. « If any one touches one of their eggs, » says the naturalist Albin, « the red-start leaves its brood; if any one touches their young, it will let them starve or it will break their neck; this has been shown by experience more than once. » This explains the care with which the red-start is always on the look-out for crumbling ruins and deserted buildings, for there, at least, it hopes that no intruder will come to disturb it.

If delicate people are unfortunate, those that take umbrage easily are yet more to be pitied. The red-start has nothing of the familiarity of the red-breast nor of the joyous disposition of the warbler. Its disposition is, in the main, a sad one, and something of its melancholy mood has passed into its song, which always seems to be impregnated with sadness, even in the season of love and pairing. All the time the female is brooding, the male red-start remains near the nest, perched on some piece of rock or some tottering stone, and there, from the earliest hours in the morning, it will sing in a sweet voice with varied modulations, which have a faint resemblance to the melody of the nightingale.

It feeds on flies, spiders, chrysalides and small wild berries. Towards the month of October it emigrates, flying across our woods; then it is possible to catch quite a large number of red-starts in those snares of the province of Lorraine, of which I have spoken in my chapter on the Finch. It has been vainly tried to tame them. When a full-grown red-start is shut up in a cage, it lets itself starve, or it shuts itself up in obstinate silence. It is only when red-starts are imprisoned in tender youth that it is possible to tame them. This is what the parents foresee without doubt, and in their hatred of servitude, with a courage worthy of the ancient Romans, they pitilessly destroy those of their children that a profane hand has touched, prefering to see them dead rather than dishonoured by bondage.

Although the propensities of the blue-breast lean also towards solitude, yet its disposition is not quite so shy. It has the same habits and the same instincts as its brother the red-breast. It only differs from the latter by the delicate blue tint which covers its throat, at the place where the former wears a breast-plate of orange-tinted red. Under this blue neck, edged with black, fawn-coloured plumage is seen on both birds; the ashy tints of the back, the reddish shade of the tail-feathers are the same both on the red-breast and the blue-breast.

Their manner of chosing their dwelling alone distinguishes the habits of these two warblers. Whereas the red-breast dwells in the depths of woods, the blue-breast remains on the outskirts, preferring damp meadows, marshy river banks, where osier grows in great abundance as well as those decorative reeds that are called cat's tails. There, they spend the fine season, living in couples, building their nests in the willows or between the tufts of osier. They have the same love for water as the red-breast, and they bathe frequently. You can meet them on slimy banks, searching for worms and insects, running

THE RED-START

about with quick movements, wide-awake eyes and turned-up tail.

The female blue-breast builds her nest in summer and constructs it of interwoven grasses, generally kept together by the reeds and osier, in the midst of which it is built. At pairing-time, the male takes its flight upwards, fluttering and singing its strain. Then it descends, turning about with the agility of the warbler, and ever chirping and twittering it swings to and fro on some flexible reed. Its chirp is very sweet in pairing-time, but it turns into rather a vulgar cry as soon as the season of courtship and love is over. The young ones are of a blackish brown hue in the beginning; the delicate blue shade of the throat appears only later, after the first moulting, and it is even said that in grown birds this beautiful colour fades in a state of captivity.

As the summer wears on, the blue-breasts approach gardens and orchards where they find savoury fruit in abundance. The vicinity of man does not frighten them. They become familiar enough to be looked at and admired at leisure, whilst they are picking the elder-berries, of which they are extremely fond. Their taste for that juicy fruit becomes fatal to them and they are frequently the victims of their greediness. The ripe berries of the elder-tree serve as a bait for bird-catchers who use a bird-call and who set lime-twigs for them on the skirts of woods. In the province of Alsace and in the Vosges mountains, many unfortunate blue-breasts are caught in this manner at the time of passage. Bird-catchers are without pity for their prettiness, without mercy for the rare, delicate shade of their breast, and they add this meagre prey to the chaplet of red-breasts, warblers and green-finches, which are destined to expire in the frying-pan. It is in an iron pan, called *coquille*, that the bird-catchers of Lorraine fry this delicious bird with tempting pieces of bacon, and compose a delicate roast that all epicures delight in.

THE BULLFINCH

This is a bird that understands
Full well the art of dining;
Stout beak has he, and knowing eye,
So brown and bright and shining.

When, dinner done, he cleans his beak
(Stained by some spicy berry)
On bark of some o'ersheltering tree,
How bright those eyes and merry!

Plump, clad in black and red, he has
    An air of cogitation,
Like some fat prelate after lunch
    Absorbed in meditation.

Soft is his song, as if he were —
    (Am I the bird maligning?)
— Were dreaming of his favourite art,
    I mean, the art of dining.

THE BULLFINCH

Spending a winter in the country, I had a bullfinch to keep me company in my retirement. It had been caught in its nest towards the end of the preceding spring and had had time enough to get accustomed to its bondage. Neither its development nor its good humour were any the worse for the domestic life it was obliged to lead. It was of the size of an ordinary sparrow. Its thick, hard, black bill was slightly bent, its nut-coloured eyes had a lovely expression, and the colours of its plumage were as bright as ever. The top of its head, the outlines of its bill and the beginning of its neck were of a fine black lustre, which set off all the more the red tint of the throat, the chest and the top of the stomach; the nape of the neck and the back had ash-coloured tints, which contrasted beautifully with the light purple, red spotted wings and the dark purple of the large tail feathers.

It was of a merry mood and had the most remarkable musical aptitude. Left in freedom, the bullfinch is only an ordinary singer. It has hardly more than three notes : a very pure whistle, then a rather hoarse warble, degenerating into a falsetto ; but the honest peasant who had undertaken the training of my particular bird, had succeeded, by dint of patience, in teaching it softer and more varied sounds. My bullfinch gave a penetrating accent to its short musical phrases, a certain softened expression, which charmed my solitude and made it dear to me. The winter was very severe. The snow would drift against the windows and settle there in white mounds ; at other times, the west wind and rain storms would beat furiously against the doors and windows of my dwelling. Neither the bullfinch nor I cared for the inclemency of the season. A bright fire was crackling in the fire place ; I had an ample supply of interesting books ; my friend had abundance of hempseed, salad and biscuits ; we spent happy days indeed in our small study, with its smoky crossbeams and its white-washed walls.

Excepting at bed-time or at night, my companion never remained shut up in its cage. The door of its prison was always open, and it took advantage of this to roam about the room, ever humming or singing. Sometimes it would perch on the pole of my bed-curtain, or it would settle near the window, very inquisitive as to what was going on outside. There, in the muddy, snowy street, a peasant would pass by, beating the pavement with his wooden shoes, or else a cart would drive past our house, splashing our window-panes with mud, and we could distinguish two or three peasant-women between the stave-sides of the cart, squatting under their blue cotton umbrellas; or else, school-children would rush out of school, making a great noise and splashing in the muddy puddles of water. The bullfinch would consider all this with pretty hitchings of its head, and at times it would particularly express its interest by some light sounds: twi! twi! twi! Sometimes too, when I was completely absorbed in my reading, it would flutter about me and finally alight on my head, where it seemed to take great pleasure in disarranging my hair.

In the evening I went out generally for my dinner and usually came home rather late. As soon as the bullfinch heard me open the door, it would wake up and was always sure to welcome me by a sweet chirping. This seemed almost to be a sort of friendly reproach for having left it alone and having remained out so late. Then, having rattled out all its grief and sadness, it would put its head under its wing; I undressed and we both fell soundly asleep; but early in the morning, it was he who awakened me by a joyous greeting. The bull-finch seemed to invite me to leave my couch, to light the fire and to fill its manger.

In this manner, we spent our winter most pleasantly; then March and its storms and showers melted the snow; the first violets, daffodils, and sweet scented wood-ruff peeped out in the garden; we could now open our window and inhale with rapture the first balmy breezes of spring.

Spring is the season when in our mountainous regions wild bullfinches begin to fly about in couples. They pair in April and build their nests in hedges. These are made of moss on the outside, of feathers on the inside; the female lays five or six bluish-white eggs spotted with violet on this soft bed. When the young ones are hatched and sufficiently feathered, the father and mother take them across the country, sometimes to blooming vines, sometimes to orchards filled with cherries, or else they fly about the skirts of a wood. The whole family leads this sort of vagrant life until the latter end of autumn, picking at ears of corn, devouring the fruit of the sloe-tree, as well as blackberries and dog-wood, disbudding aspen-trees, alders and sorbs; whistling, calling and answering each other, intoxicating themselves with air and sunshine.

I do not know whether my bullfinch (a male) had a

THE BULLFINCH

vague sort of inner presentiment of all these things, but as April was making Nature green and the air was getting warmer, it became more restless and more turbulent. It would leave its cage more willingly, fluttering impatiently about the room, hanging on the window-sill or beating lightly against the panes with its bill.

Surely some mysterious instinct had been telling my companion about the budding hedges and the free bullfinches who were making love to each other in the pleasant sunlight. It cared no longer for its food, although it was generally very much of an epicure; it disdained its hempseed and biscuit; it had only one object in view: the window; it would spend hours there as if in a dream, looking at the trees, whose new leaves the wind was shaking, and which appeared just above the opposite wall beyond. Then another fit of frenzy would seize it; it would pick again at the window-panes, repeatedly uttering a low cry which seemed to say: Why do you not let me out? Why do you not let me out?

One fine morning, finding the window ajar, it flew away while my back was turned.

Dazzled at first by the sunlight and not accustomed to the open air, it did not fly far. At a distance of a few yards from the house, there was a heap of manure in which about a dozen hens were scratching. There the bullfinch halted to make use of its liberty by hunting for worms in this fruitful ground. But it had not counted on the intolerant, quarrelsome disposition of these shrews. At the sight of the intruder that came to pilfer on their estates, the hens flew into a great rage. In a second my poor bullfinch was surrounded, worried, picked at and plucked by their sharp bills.

Leaning out of my window, I had followed my fugitive with my eyes, and I understood the danger it was in. I jumped out of the window, ran to the spot, but it was too late. — Bruised, plucked and bleeding, my poor little companion lay motionless on the dung heap, whilst those harpies were yet worrying it with their bills; — when I succeeded at last in pulling it out of their clutches, my poor bullfinch was dead.

THE THRUSH

Now is the tale of August's wealth
   In golden glories told,
And all the laden vineyard glows
   With purple grapes and gold.

From vat or winepress duly filled
   With juices of the vine
There comes on every breeze that blows
   The drowsy scent of wine.

With laughter loud and kisses long
   Through all the leafy way,
In alleys of the clustering vine
   Do men and maidens stay.

Blended with voices of the birds
   Who steal the grapes and sing
Their loud and joyous merriment
   Makes all the vineyard ring.

And lo! the thrush who loudly sings
   On topmost wreath of vine
With juice of grape and joy of heart
   Is drunk as if with wine.

THE THRUSH

Five years ago, on a beautiful day in September, I was descending a hollow road in Brittany, going from the village of Briantais to that of Saint-Jouan, one of those broad, grass-grown foot-paths which are so frequently found in that province. On both sides of the road the slopes rose like two green walls, planted with chesnut-trees and pollards. The wheels of the carts that had passed on this road had left deep ruts where the rain had settled in pools, and in that damp, moist soil, the pink flowers of the lesser centaury appear in full bloom.

It was perhaps eight o'clock in the morning; I was listening in the balmy freshness of early autumn to the parish bells ringing for mass, whilst thrushes were singing in the juniper trees of the moor. At the same time the salt breezes that blew from beyond the sloping declivity told me the sea was near.

I was just about climbing over a fence made of boughs when I heard some steps behind me, and turning round, I perceived an early riser who was fond of walking, coming in my direction. He appeared to be about thirty; he was dressed in a suit of dark blue cloth, wore a round felt hat and looked like a well-to-do country gentleman; his dress was even too elaborate for that early morning hour, and his drawn features, his eyes circled with black, his hooked nose pinched at its extremity, his leady complexion, all seemed to indicate that he had passed a sleepless night. Not being very well acquainted with the topogaphy of the locality, I took advantage of this unexpected meeting to ask him whether I was on the right road to Saint-Jouan.

He answered in the affirmative and told me he was going the same way himself, adding : « I shall be happy to show you the shortest way, as I am going home and anxious to get to bed ».

He noticed doubtlessly an expression of surprise in my face, for he added smilingly : « You are astonished that I should go to bed when others rise? It is quite natural; I spent the night at the Casino of Saint-Malo; the game of *baccarat* was very animated, and we only left the gaming table at early dawn ».

I considered him more attentively: he had indeed the countenance of a gambler. His grey eyes were glistening feverishly and contrasted with the impassibility of the rest of his features. As we were walking along, a thrush began to sing. The grave notes of its song alternated with low, chirping, shrill flourishes; my companion lifted his head suddenly and listened to the familiar strain.

« That's a young thrush », muttered he, « a pretty bird, my good sir! it is clearing its throat with the fruit of the juniper-tree and that softens its voice. I am fond of hearing that song on the moor..... It is a fetich and it brings me good luck..... If I had heard it yesterday when I was going to the Casino, I should perhaps have had better luck! But instead of that I am going home completely plucked. — Fortunately I am not easily discouraged and shall make up to-morrow for to-day's ill luck! »

The thrush continued throwing its trills into the air, and the gamester, standing on the grassy declivity, stopped again to listen.

« I know that particular bird, said he; it has built its nest on the lower branches of an oak-tree; I caught it the other day brooding, for with these birds, it is the male who broods, so as to let the female rest! It is a most excellent father and husband ! » My companion sighed again . « I noticed this thrush », he continued, « on account of its black eyes and the orange coloured tint of its wings; these two traits distinguish it from the red-wing or wind-thrush. Just as I was bending over the nest, the bird flew away; — I ought not to have startled it, it has brought me ill-luck ! »

We had now reached the entrance to a long avenue of beech-trees ; at the other extremity of which we could perceive the gate of a manor-house built in the architectural style of the time of Louis XIII.

« This is the road that leads to Saint-Jouan », said my companion, « and I am now at home. Good morning to you, my dear sir ! »

We separated, and I saw him disappear slowly under the shady arch of the beeches. — At Saint-Jouan I questioned the inn-keeper about him and I heard that the avenue of beeches led to the manor of « La Crochais », belonging to a certain M. de Trelivan.

The following week at the Casino I again met the owner of « La Crochais ». He was sitting at a *baccarat* table and holding the bank. While dealing he was biting his lips and drops of perspiration were standing on his brow. A quarter of an hour later, he gathered up what he had won, picked up a pile of gold and rose from his seat. He recognized me immediately and came up to me, saying:

« It's all right. I am making up for my losses of the

THE THRUSH

other day.... You see, it is necessary not to give in....
and besides, added he in a low voice, I heard the thrush
singing on the moor this evening, its song was never mer-
rier. It's a pretty bird, sir! While I was listening to its
song, I was saying to myself: « I shall have luck to-night! »
and so far really, I have no reason to be dissatisfied! »

I left Saint-Malo on the following day. I came back
this year, and the other day took a drive to Dinan, following the left bank of the Rance. On the road, one of
the bolts of the pole of my carriage having dropped, we
were obliged to halt going down hill. « Fortunately there
is a farrier at Saint-Jouan », said the driver ; « if you would
be kind enough sir, to walk as far as that, it will take only
five minutes to have the pole repaired ».

The name of Saint-Jouan awoke a slumbering recol-
lection in my mind. I recognized the landscape that I had
perceived years ago : the avenue of beeches, the slate-
covered roof of the manor, buried in the shining verdure
of the chesnut trees, and the moor where the thrushes were
singing as formerly. To the left of the road, at a turning,
I noticed a grey granite cross erected on a low hill; above
this cross maple trees were shaking their silvery leaves.
« Is there any one buried here? » I asked of the driver.

« Yes sir, the owner of « La Crochais », that manor on
your right, a certain M. de Trelivan ». Trelivan ! the name
was sufficient to bring the past back to my mind. I saw
again before me my companion of yore with his robust

frame, his erect carriage, his feverish eye, stopping on the moor to listen to the song of the thrush.

« He blew out his brains on this very spot, sir, continued the driver, you see he was a gambler ; he had just lost some enormous sums at the Casino, and had a wife and children. One morning, as he was coming home, he sat down yonder, facing his avenue, and blew out his brains ! A great pity, to be sure ! a magnificent looking man, and so merry when he had good luck ! Sometimes, when I drove him to Saint-Malo, he made me stop on the road to listen to the thrush. He used to say that it brought him luck ! It must surely be, that the thrush had'nt sung that morning ! »

THE SWALLOW

When the winter days are ended,
And the trees put on their leaves,
As her wont is, comes the swallow,
Twittering gaily in the eaves.

And when summer days are gone,
With tireless wing and dauntless heart
As their wont is, to the southward,
Do the swallow kind depart.

As I watch the parting swallow,
On her way to distant lands
I would fain that I might follow,
To the desert and its sands.

Ah to break the bound that holds me!
Ah! to set my spirit free!
Free to wander like the swallow,
Over continent and sea!

THE SWALLOW

 I remember one evening having witnessed the departure of swallows from a corner window, looking out on the solitary small square of a country town. One of the sides of the square was entirely occupied by an old mansion; its balconies, cornices and friezes offering numberless resting places to the future travellers.

During the last few days I had noticed an unusual coming and going among the swallows. They were flying about restlessly, with a very busy look. Some would dart down the whole length of the street, describing long circuts, throwing out cries of appeal, then reappearing at the other end of the street, bringing up many new-comers, which like quarter-masters, would inspect every corner and then disappear likewise. Every morning the band increased considerably. You would have thought they were experimenting on the preliminaries of departure, and that the messengers had been ordered to indicate to all the place of final congregation.

Evidently the collective departure of these birds necessitates a number of private meetings and an agreement prepared long beforehand. Even if we admit certain mysterious presentiments, it would be absurd to believe that instinct alone, so to say mechanical, could make all the swallows of one region congregate together at the same time and the same place. This displacement of a whole population of birds can only be explained by a series of rather complex reasoning and by a special sort of language, establishing prompt communication between individuals of the same species. Who assumes the responsibility of the meeting? who chooses the hour of departure and the place of congregating? Probably the elders of the tribe, those who have had most experience.

It is well known that swallows come back faithfully every year to the same quarters and the same nest. Therefore, there must exist in every borough, in every town, some old patriarchs well acquainted with all variations of climate, with all local resources, with the roads to be taken, and who, having the presentiment of the coming hour of migration, will agree about the place of meeting; then, they will disperse in the country all around, to inform the whole clan. Many naturalists noticed long ago that swallows have a peculiar cry for the circumstance, which they call « the cry of assembly ».

These preparations interested me exceedingly. I could watch them from our garret window, where precisely two swallows had built their hemispheric nest of straw and gravel, which they regularly occupied every year. I had witnessed the return of our guests for the last three years, having watched intently the process of brooding and the training of the young ones. Once even, after having read a book on swallows, I had caught one of the parents by means of a net spread over the orifice of the nest and I had tied a green silk string to its foot. How happy I was the following spring, to see in the nest the same swallow having yet a bit of the green thread tied to its foot! This circumstance redoubled my interest in these birds which had come back from afar to a dormer window in our humble dwelling !

Swallows had for me that marvelous attraction that draws us towards people who have travelled in foreign countries. Their return was a sign of coming spring; their departure always left me with an aching heart; it told me that the end of my holidays was drawing near.....

Emotion mingled with regret, as if I were witnessing the last act of some pathetic tragedy, while I was watching their last gatherings.

During these preparatory evolutions the power, the strength and the elasticity of their wings seemed to have increased. It was a delight to see their fluttering in the open air. There they displayed all the resources of their art of flying: turning and turning about again and again, changing their direction at every minute and exercising themselves to soar high in the air. You could see that having to accomplish a long sea-voyage, they encouraged each other and tried the strength of their wings, so as not to carry any stragglers with them. It is even probable, that, if during these preparatory exercises any swallow had revealed some weakness of constitution, it would have been pitilessly left behind. Besides, this is the manner of proceeding of all migratory birds that travel in flocks — An Austrian officer told me that he had seen storks congregate together on the wide plains of Hungary at the minute of starting. For hours they would describe long circles so as to put their strength to a trial. If one of the storks, too old or too ill, lost its strength and dropped down, immediately the whole flock darted on the poor creature and killed it pitilessly.

No such tragic event accompanied the departure of my swallows, and I had no such execution to witness.

One September afternoon, I saw them arrive in great

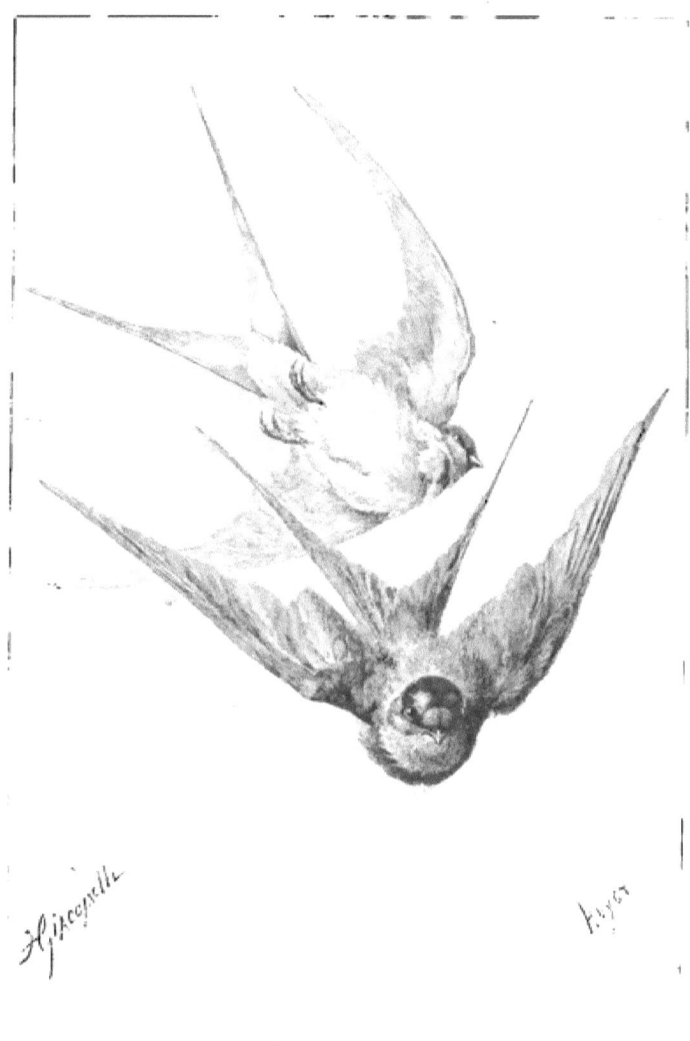

THE SWALLOW

flocks in the square. The weather was fine and grape gathering and vintage had begun. Merry sunshine was bathing the dew-covered roofs and at both extremities of the street I could perceive the vine-covered slopes of our hills. From all the streets near by swallows were issuing. They would turn a minute in the sky, then they would perch on the window-sills and cornices of the houses. The supports of the balconies and the friezes were soon covered by a long line of small black heads, nodding softly with low melodious chirping. Now and then, one swallow would leave the line and at a single flight would survey the front of the ranks, as if to make sure that every thing was in order and the troup complete. No, not yet. At every instant stragglers were coming up hastily; they were received with impatient cries from the birds of the flock; then, with yet more noise and tumult, they would draw up closer so as to make room for the new-comers.

After a little while a profound silence began to reign among the flock — an almost solemn silence. The sun was already lower down and sending oblique rays into the street; the shadow of the hills was lengthening on the town. Suddenly, at a single flight, the troup of swallows took wing and ascended, their wings fluttering and quivering with confusion and agitation. For one second the sky was darkened by this black battalion hovering above the square; then the swallows, forming a long winding line, took their flight towards the south and disappeared in the mists which overcast the horizon.

When I turned my eyes again to the ground, the whole town appeared to me sad and lonely. I remained a long while standing at my window, thrilled with that sensation of sadness and solitude which follows the departure of those whom we love

THE RED-BREAST

Twit! Tweet! Tweet! Tweet! Daybreaks,
And Robin Redbreast wakes.
Still sleep the quails in the corn
But love within thy nest
Wakes up betimes, Redbreast,
    Greeting the morn.

Right early, too, in spring
Thy love wakes up to sing.
Thy nest braves April showers,
Built when the March winds blow,
And when the spring days show
    Their earliest flowers.

    Love is not marred or made
    By change of sun or shade;
    With you, 't is constant, whether
    Dark be the skies or blue;
    Love is the same for you
        In any weather.

THE RED-BREAST

 Thomas Carlyle used to be fond of relating that in the beginning of his career he had been obliged to live a long time in the turmoil of a big city, where he had met with nothing but annoyance. One day, as he was coming home, morally worn out and discouraged, he suddenly heard a band of larks sending up their joyous strain from the corn-fields, just as he had formerly heard them chirp in his father's farms; this unexpected music then cheered him greatly and gave him new courage to fight the battle of life.

This evening, I have had a similar emotion, sweet and yet melancholy, while I was listening to the song of the red-breasts in the beeches of a neighbouring park. Birds have that peculiarity of always appearing to be *the same* that we have heard before. Years pass away, we grow old, we see our friends die or disappear, we see revolutions change the face of things in the world, our illusions vanish one by one, and yet, in the trees of the orchards or the beeches in the woods, the birds that we have known in childhood repeat the same melodious call, modulate the same musical phrases with the same voice, apparently as young as ever. Time never seems to touch them, and as they hide out of sight when they die, as we never witness their agony, we can easily imagine that we are yet in the presence of the same songsters that charmed us in early youth.

Be that as it will, the red-breasts to which I have been listening to-night were warbling their song with the same tender and caressing expression as when I was young. They were skipping about merrily and familiarly quite near me in the reddening branches, and I could distinctly perceive their bright black eyes, their brown heads and their breast with its beautiful reddish orange tint. The aspect of the bushes, covered with blackberries, the particular scent of the woods at the latter end of autumn, the charm of the beautiful red tints of that season of the year, added to the hallucination. I thought that the golden days of yore had come back, when, during the summer holidays, I would lie on my back, stretched on the grass on the outskirts of a wood, building magnificent castles in the air, whilst listening to the appealing cry of the birds of passage. In those days, I would dream — my heart beating joyously all the while — of my coming youth, of the smiling perspectives of the future, whilst the red-breasts, with their song, were warbling an approving accompaniment to my reveries.

To-night, I hear them again. The setting sun is just as magnificent — and yet its splendour is not quite the same as of yore. The tints and outlines of the landscape seem to be veiled with some melancholy mist. The time of maturity has come with disillusion, bitter experience, thwarted hopes. At half a yard's distance, there where the water is greenish in the cisterns, a red-breast was singing, perched on a wild rose bush above my head. The bird was looking at me familiarly with its arch black eye, seeming to say to me:

« Well! old comrade, you have indeed grown old! »

You, you are ever the same, oh friendly red-breast! Your breast has yet that fine colour of ripe sorb to which you owe your name! At early dawn, you awake, you, the earliest riser among birds, and sing your melodious *tireli*. All day long, in the depths of damp woods, you are searching for food under the dead leaves. On Saint-Albin's day, when the meadows are yet covered with hoar-frost, you bravely select the place of your future nest ; you begin to warble, in order to charm your mate, and as your heart is as true and as faithful as it is warm and passionate, you have not many deceptions in love. In the warm nest you have woven of moss and grass, your large family is slumbering peacefully; when you leave your dwelling to search for food, you cover the entrance of the nest with a dry leaf, like a prudent landlord who closes the latch of his door before going out, and you take wing with a quiet mind, having no care and no uneasiness.

When autumn comes, and haw, sorbs and dog-wood redden the hedges, you change your bill of fare, and you begin to live on juicy, perfumed fruit. Your throat then acquires a fresh suppleness, and your song new beauty and power. Leaves fall from the trees, but the first colds of winter will not frighten you; you will only fly nearer to human dwellings. It seems that you regret to leave us, and often, in the month of November, the first soft snow will take you by surprise, and you will hammer with your bill against some bright window, asking unceremoniously for shelter and food.

To be sure, you do not escape the common lot, and you will grow old just as we all do; only to us it does not seem so, and we do not perceive that you are changing. We see red-breasts hopping and skipping about at the same places as formerly; we hear your autumnal song, and it seems to us that we are yet hearing the same bird. They say that you are spared the decrepitude of old age, and

THE RED BREAST

that generally you die suddenly, struck by a fit of apoplexy. That is another of the privileges of your destiny. As Montaigne says : « The deadest deaths are the best. » On some evening in spring or summer, after too substantial a meal, or too long a feast of love, you will receive your death-blow. Dead leaves will cover your small body, just as they formerly covered your nest, and dying, you can still imagine that you are lying in your cradle.

Our lot is not so happy as yours, oh robin red-breast ! Our life, less uniform than yours, is fuller of deceiving complications.

> . . . . A changeful infinite
> It spreads before our eyes like some vast plain
> Where fairy magic spreads for our delight
> The varying witchery of its mystic train.
>
> There may we roam, too, lost in wonderment,
> To choose among the myriad opening flowers :
> Amazed with beauty, afar, we miss the scent
> Of buds already grasped by hands of ours.

But although our life be interwoven with honeysuckles or briers, although it be entangled with numberless black threads, amongst which glisten just a few golden ones, it must yet finish like thine, oh robin red-breast ! not quite so suddenly perchance, with more ups and downs, with a more lingering old age.... nevertheless, it must come to an end. Like thee, we must sleep in the dark earth, and nothing will remain of our individuality, of which we were so proud, but a remembrance, which lasts more or less and disappears entirely as years roll on. For a short while our friends will speak of us with a tear and a sigh; then all regrets will vanish. Those who have wept on our grave will be consoled, and then disappear likewise, and insensibly and silently forgetfulness will heap dry leaves over our individuality as over thine! All will have forgotten the way to our grave, but butterflies and the birds of the skies. It will be a lucky chance indeed, oh robin red-breast, if one of thy brethren will come to warble there his friendly strain, the self same song, ever young and ever beautiful!

THE TITMOUSE

Dearest, since budding April hangs with green
The boughs of all the neighbouring bushes, see
Here let us build our mossy nest, between
The budding branches of this willow tree.

Must needs a cradle softly lined and warm
Be woven of straws, and moss, and down, my sweet
To screen thy precious eggs from cold or harm;
Here will I bring thee dainty food to eat.

While thou dost brood, until, e'er end of spring,
Thy warmth of heart will at the last compel
Our younglings, helpless things and twittering,

To break their way from protecting shell
We are but two to sing the praise of Spring
But twelve or so will praise the Autumn well."

THE TITMOUSE FAMILY

During the first rainy days of October, when windows however yet remain open, I could hear the low warbling of the titmice in the pines and firs of the garden. They had come there in troops ever since Michaelmas, and they were actively engaged in picking spindle-trees, yews and larches. Ever alert, they flutter about from one group of trees to another, skipping on the branches, turning the leaves, climbing along the bark, suspending themselves with their back downwards, so as to be able to pick more easily the crevices in the bark, where they know that worms and insects hide their chrysalis.

All these titmice differ in colour, size and general

appearance; still they offer certain general characteristics which do not allow us to have the slightest doubt about their common parentage. They all have a short, cone-shaped bill which is slightly flattened on the sides and covered up to the nostrils with small feathers which bristle easily and give an impertinent expression to their physiognomy. All titmice too have very robust muscles in the neck; their skull is very thick; they also have much strength in the muscles of their feet and toes; this explains the suppleness and agility of their wonderful gymnastic feats, when they destroy caterpillars on the branches, pick hard seeds and pierce the shell of hazelnuts. It has even been said that they take advantage of the sharpness of their bill, which can be compared to a blade of steel, in order to pierce the skulls of small birds when they find them either dead or weakened by illness, so as to feast on their brains. Ordinarily however, titmice are satisfied with more innocent food; they live chiefly on caterpillars, eggs of butterflies, but also on hazelnuts, beech-nuts, walnuts, and in general on all kinds of oil-seed.

During the fine season they live in the depths of hilly woods, but as soon as the first cold sets in and the first snow falls on the mountains, they emigrate towards cultivated plains and draw nearer to inhabited regions. Nearly all titmice are remarkable for their talent in nest-building, which is truly extraordinary in such small birds. They employ in the construction of their nest choice material, such as small blades of grass, flexible roots, soft silky moss, bits of wool, feathers and vegetable down, and they use their bill in a most skilful manner for interweaving, rounding off, smoothing and shaping these materials so various in texture and in form.

Titmice are all very prolific. Most of the females lay as many as fifteen or even eighteen eggs. Their family instinct is also very much developed. Both males and females display untiring zeal in feeding their large progeniture and unequalled energy in defending it against the attacks of owls and other rapacious birds. In the main, the disposition of titmice is naturally violent, daring and warlike.

It is doubtless due to their intrepidity and quarrelsome temper developed by the obligation of being ever on the defensive, that titmice have sometimes been accused of slyness, cunning and ferocity. But on the contrary it seems to me that we ought to admire the courage with which these birdlings fight the hard struggle for existence. Their fondness for live flesh has often been cast at them as a reproach, live flesh which they tear with their nails just like the shrike and the raven; but one is apt to forget that their small body is only a bundle of muscles and nerves and needs very substantial food to resist the wear and tear of life. Their constitution demands the assimilation of a great quantity of animal food. Why do we not cast the same reproach at the nightingale which also lives on bleeding flesh?

As to the cunning of titmice, is not that a light fault indeed in this wee bird which disappears in the bigness of the great forest, where it is constantly obliged to defend itself and family against the attacks of such marauders as the night-owl and the squirrel? Pheasants too are sly and cunning, but this takes away none of their solid and valiant merits. If perchance, pressed by famine a titmouse pierces the skull of a dead or dying bird, it is not we, who are such ferocious hunters and anglers, who have the right to cast this into its teeth or to accuse it of a crime.

To eat or to be eaten is a terrible dilemma, which does not allow him who is driven into it, to give himself up to excessive sensibility. I should like to see those moralists who accuse titmice of cruelty, thrown without food or clothing into a wilderness, and under the necessity of getting their food by the strength of their nails!...

The truth is that titmice are very sociable. Whether they have a taste for society, or whether the sense of their weakness makes them congregate together, is more than we can say; but it is sure that they are fond of the society of their equals and take their flight in larger or smaller troops. When perchance some accident has separated them, they quickly utter their call and are promptly reunited.

Whilst I was meditating on the faults and qualities of titmice, I happened to be an eye-witness to a sample of those beautiful relations which are established among the different members of this family.

THE TITMOUSE

In the pines and firs, in the hawthorn and barberry bushes already stripped of their leaves which I could see from my window, all the different species of titmice were represented, seeming to live in perfect harmony. They formed various groups, all very busy and very restless. To class them all by name one by one would require a numbering almost after the fashion of Homer.

There was *the great black-headed titmouse* easily recognised by its square build, its black hood and black breast-plate. When the weather is unsettled and it is going to rain, it utters a cry which is like the grinding of a file on a piece of iron, whence one of its French surnames: *la serrurière* (the locksmith). But generally it has a pleasing warble, especially in the season of love. It builds its nest in the holes of walls, in the trunks of trees, sometimes also in coal-sheds abandoned by coal-burners.

Beside the great black-headed titmouse, the *blue titmouse* is very busy, the prettiest, the boldest, the bravest of the family; — it is a lovely bird with its delicate head covered by a blue hood, its bluish wings, its white cheeks and its dark blue collar. This bird is the most terrible destroyer of caterpillars. It has been calculated that it eats daily half an ounce of eggs of butterflies.

Then comes the *ash-coloured titmouse* or *nun*, which stores away seed in its hole and makes war on wasps; — then the *great titmouse*, which weaves its mossy nest in a marvellous manner, and suspends it on the boughs of trees just like the gold-hammer; — lastly, the *long-tailed titmouse*, with its rapid, elegant flight which can only be compared to the shooting of an arrow.

All these minute folks were hopping, skipping and springing about and warbling peacefully in the green boughs. Suddenly the whole troup took wing with a startled cry; at the same time the report of a gun was heard. I recognised there one of those finely characteristic traits of *man*, that mild and benevolent animal who is so very much shocked by the ferocity of titmice. Fortunately these birdlings are wise and experienced; they had foreseen the shot and had taken wing in time.

THE WREN

Over the waves and far away
The birds are winging their way,
Seeking a country new
Afar o'er the waters blue.
'T is winter; they dare not stay;
They're over the waves and away.

But one little bird is bold
To dare the rain and the cold,
The hail and the falling snow
And winds that bluster and blow.
The big birds have fled from the cold,
But one little bird is bold.

Little wren with the golden crest,
A brave heart beats in your breast.
On boughs where the hoarfrosts cling
You sit in the woods and sing.
May gladness dwell in your nest,
Little wren with the golden crest!

THE WREN AND THE TROGLODYTE

I found one day a marvelously constructed nest in the boughs of a larch tree. Imagine a large ball, delicately woven of moss and gossamer threads, wadded inside with the warmest and softest down, gathered from the catkins of poplars, the ripe tufts of thistles and the cottony seed of the willow herb. This soft nest, into which one could only penetrate on one side by a narrow opening, was the work of the golden-crested wren, that liliputian bird, the smallest of our European birds.

The wren is yet smaller and more delicate than its cousin the troglodyte, with which it is often confounded, although the two birds differ in manners, plumage and song. The troglodyte is about an inch longer than the golden-crowned wren; its plumage is shaded off from dark brown to black, like that of the woodcock; its tail is constantly turned up like a plume of feathers; it sings moreover a merry, melodious strain. It builds its nest anywhere, sometimes close to the ground, on some bough covered with dense foliage; sometimes under the thatched roof of some lone cottage, and even sometimes on the hut of a coal-burner or maker of wooden shoes, who carry on their trade in the heart of the forest. Their nest consists of a ball of moss, shapeless on the outside, but very skilfully lined with feathers on the inside. In this soft nest the female lays nine or ten eggs of a dull whitish colour spotted with red at the broader end. As soon as the young ones are feathered, the family scatters and disperses in the forest.

The troglodyte lives in secluded retirement, in bushes and thickets. There it flutters about until night has set in, and it is, with the red-breast and the blackbird, one of the last birds whose song is heard after the sun has set. It is not shy, and the neighbourhood of man does not annoy it in the least. I remember having met a troglodyte in the forest of Compiègne, which was fluttering about between the entangled branches of a sloe-tree, and it did not seem at all disquieted by my presence. It went on humming, singing with a clear voice, turning up its small tail, agitating its wings, and passing through the thickets and briers with the vivacity of a lizard. When winter is drawing near, this small birdling remains in the neighbourhood of farms and orchards, ever singing merrily, in spite of cold and in spite of snow. « It is never melancholy, says Belon; it is ever ready to sing; one is sure to hear it at morn and at night from a distance, and generally in winter time, and its song then is scarcely less loud than that of the nightingale. »

The bird to which the troglodyte bears the closest resemblance, in voice and in habits, is the small willow-wren or pewet. The pewet is of the same size as the wren; it has also the same plumage, with the exception of the crest; but it has the habits and general bearing of the troglodyte. Like the latter, it feeds on worms and flies, which it pursues with astonishing vivacity. The female lays generally five or six white eggs, with russet-coloured spots. The young ones do not leave their mossy bed till they are able to fly. In Autumn, the pewet imitates its cousin the troglodyte; it abandons the large forests and begins to flutter near orchards. Its song consists of long shrill notes, with varied modulations; it begins with a sort of syncopated murmur; then come some silvery notes, clear and distinct; lastly, a very sweet, sustained warbling, which, especially in Autumn, finishes off in a loud whistle: tuit! tuit! and which is like the characteristic signature of this diminutive virtuoso.

The golden-crested wren, on the contrary, scarcely

ever warbles excepting at the time of brooding; at all other times, it utters only a sort of single shrill cry which is very much like that of the grasshopper. But if it does not shine by its song, it makes up for this imperfection by wearing on its forehead the badge of royalty. Its plain brown plumage is set off by a beautiful gold coloured crown. This crest consists of moveable feathers which the wren, by means of certain muscles in the head, can raise or lower at pleasure. The crest is edged with black; a white line at its basis, a black trait on both sides of the eyes, mark yet more the courageous and resolute mien of this miniature monarch.

And indeed the golden-crowned wren is full of vivacity and energy: there is not a bird who undertakes more bravely the struggle for existence. In summer's sun, in winter's cold it skips with intrepidity from tree to bush, from bush to blade of grass, shelling the yellow grain of fennel seed, clearing the needles of the larch tree, picking in the crevices of the bark of willows to find larvae of insects or eggs of butterflies.

It is exceedingly fond of biting off young leaves from the boughs of the trees of the pine family: pines, fir trees, juniper trees, which conceal a whole world of larvae and eggs between their needles. The wren is a master in the art of destroying caterpillars. It has been calculated that a golden-crested wren can devour yearly three millions of eggs and of chrysalides.

THE WREN

It differs in this from the troglodyte : it pursues its occupations, followed by its whole family, with order and method. The whole band flies from one tuft of shoot to the other, in a certain direction determined by a special instinct of migration. An ornithologist, who is known as a close observer of nature, M. de la Blanchère, has told us in his interesting book about *Useful and noxious birds*, that he had succeeded in knowing well by which side a golden-crested wren had entered into a forest, and also in which regions of the forest he would unfailingly meet these little birdlings all winter long.

The golden-crested wren is fond of large trees. It suspends its nest beneath some forest pine tree, in whose boughs the wind sings such melodious strains, or else beneath the majestic fir of the Vosges, all bordered with lichen. In this nest, rocked by the waves of the big forest, the female lays from seven to eleven yellowish brown eggs, about the size of green peas. Now-a-days, only low people or kings can afford the luxury of such large families.

In its small body, the golden-crowned wren combines at the same time royal and plebeian blood. By its size, its industrious habits and its good humour, it belongs to the people; but it wears a crown and reigns in the forest in a fashion of its own. It enjoys a sort of mysterious, intangible royalty, which can only be compared to that of Queen Mab or to that of Oberon. In the large, sleeping forest, the golden-crowned wren represents movement and life. When the frozen brooks are silent, when not a blade of grass is moving, when the wood-cutter warms his fingers by blowing on them before taking up the hatchet, he hears suddenly a light, merry cry, and sees a lovely, diminutive apparition, crowned with a crest of gold, gliding between the bare boughs. It is the familiar spirit of the big forest, the beautiful golden-crowned wren, which laughs at the bleak north wind, and continues picking caterpillars from the juniper trees, almost buried in snow.

THE BLACKBIRD

In March sings the Blackbird, aloft sits he
In the blossom white on the damson tree,
And whistles as loud as loud can be.

In spite of the frosty meadows,
And hail that drives in the sky
And whitens the grass in the orchard,
He knows that spring is nigh.

He thinks of the juicy cherries
That summer will set on the trees,
And dreaming of loaded orchards
He fancies their scent in the breeze

Afar, like a fairy vision
He sees in the vineyard bare,
Its leaves in the autumn ruddy,
Its sweet grapes ripening there.

In March sings the Blackbird, aloft sits he
A bird as black as black can be,
In the blossom white on the damson tree.

THE BLACKBIRD

Every one knows that joyous fellow, even Parisians who have never much lived in the country, for it is the guest of all Paris gardens and squares. Every-where, in the Luxembourg and Tuileries gardens, in the Parc Monceau, you can see them skipping and hopping about in the flowerbeds or on the lawns, nimble and alert, and easily recognized by their fine shiny black costume and their yellow bill. The female almost always accompanies the male, her costume is grey; she is as discreet, reserved and silent as he is talkative

The blackbird is not a bird of passage, but a sedentary one; even in the severest cold it remains in our lands. In winter, in cities, it is fond of haunting the neighbourhood of dwellings, where, among the green boughs of the gardens, it is always sure to find shelter and some sort of food.

When the country blackbirds feel that winter is setting in, they seek a refuge in the very depths of the forest, within reach of some tepid spring, beneath some pines or juniper trees, which offer them, better board and lodging. As soon as the cold is less intense they become very merry and begin, already early in February, to utter that joyous whistle which resounds so merrily in forest thickets and parks, when chestnut catkins begin to bloom. They build their nest very early, and if the first brood does not live on account of the cold, the female is not discouraged and begins to lay her eggs a second time. They build their nest nearly even with the soil, or sometimes in the hollow of some old willow. Their nest bears a great resemblance to that of the thrush; it is made of solid masonry and woven very dexterously; a layer of clay covers it on the outside, on the inside it is lined with grass and roots, and again with soft moss. The female lays four or five bluish green eggs, spotted with rust. She broods them alone, while the male is fluttering to and fro, whistling merrily and searching at the same time for food; this he brings back to his mate after having divided it into pieces.

The disposition of the blackbird; is very jovial; it is

so to say the wag of the world of birds. It has something
of the animation and the crack spirits of a clown or a low
actor, and like these merry-makers it needs a gallery to
listen to it and to applaud it. It is very fond of society,
but prefers to the companionship of its brethren, that of
smaller birds of different species. Often, towards evening,
I have observed the manœuvres of blackbirds on the
large lawns of the Luxembourg. Each one would skip
lightly over the grass, escorted by four five familiar
sparrows, that seemed to be very proud of being admitted
into the intimacy of the fine blackbird with its hand-
some black dress. The latter, meanwhile, would skip to
and fro, with a mien of self importance and condescen-
sion; it seemed to take great pleasure in astonishing
the « small fry » which it consented to admit into its
company. It appeared to me like one of those witty wags
who are at the same time vain, noisy and vulgar, who
disdain their equals and only find themselves at ease in
the company of persons they can dazzle and over whom
they can lord it easily.

The blackbird is fond of showing himself in public;
he likes to have all the talk to himself, and makes himself everywhere at home very unceremoniously. I remember having witnessed one morning in autumn a most
amusing scene, in which a blackbird played the chief part.
On the outskirts of a vineyard, a blackbird, drunk with
grape juice, was parading near me, accompanied by half a

dozen thrushes. The wag, merrily inclined, was perched on top of one of the vine-poles giving a performance for the benefit of his merry followers. He twinkled his eyes, fluttered his wings, agitated his tail, put his head between his feet, with a grotesque mien, which greatly amused his lady spectators, very attentive to all that was going on.

And besides, autumn is a season of high glee and merry-making for the blackbird. The orchards are full of stone fruit, wild berries are abundant in the hedges, the grape-vines are loaded with grapes. Therefore, it cares no longer for worms or insects; it stuffs itself with the pulp of sweet-scented, juicy fruit. It has no other care but that of satisfying its greediness : love is no longer one of its torments, and it has become silent. It only utters a sort of ill-humoured sound, when disturbed whilst taking its dinner.

But the finest of holidays will come to an end. One by one, the fruit-trees lose their leaves and their fruit; the grapes are gathered. There is nothing more to steal on bush or hedge but a few berries on the sloe tree and in the thickets, already covered with hoar frost. Now the long days of feasting are over; the blackbird must be satisfied with less abundant fare. At the end of November, the last wild berries have disappeared with the frost... Good bye, juicy fruit.

The blackbird now retreats towards the big clumps of trees and establishes itself in its winter quarters. There,

THE BLACKBIRD

the fare is but middling and the society it meets not very amusing. The time of merry-making is over. My Lord Blackbird is obliged to come back to the diet of grub and worms, and even these are not always found in sufficient quantity. All his boon companions, being afraid of cold, have emigrated towards warmer climes. His only society are titmice, whom we know as cross-grained, peevish, and positive people; busy birds, indeed, little inclined to listen to the fooleries of the blackbird; he also finds golden-crested wrens, who being of a reserved disposition, fly from the vicinity of our big noisy blackbird.

Happily, he is a philosopher. He repeats to himself for his own benefit all his waggish tales, like an old, long forgotten actor who plays over again for himself all those scenes in which he used to be applauded in his best days. And then he consoles himself by saying to himself that bad days will pass by as well as happy ones, and that after all, winter is not everlasting. Already at the end of January he perches on the topmost branch of a fir tree and watches attentively the lengthening days and the rising temperature. On Saint-Antony's day days « lengthen the length of a monk's meal, » and at Candlemass « they lengthen an hour »; and with all that the latter end of winter is at hand. By a peculiar instinct, midst rainshowers and February storms, the blackbird knows that spring-time is near. It sees the catkins on hazel-nut trees growing longer; it sees that in the thickets the black hellebore is opening its green corollas edged with rose colour : on all sides, in every nook and corner the woods seem to say : « Spring has returned ! »

In its heart of hearts the blackbird feels it also. In its breast the desire of love is budding, just as buds are appearing on the boughs, and suddenly it begins to whistle merrily. That alert whistle which resounds in the silent, deserted forest is the first note on the fiddle which gives the signal of the ever renewed, ever enchanting symphony of spring.

www.ingramcontent.com/pod-product-compliance
Lightning Source LLC
Chambersburg PA
CBHW031815220426
43662CB00007B/663